英語訳付き

日本の神輿と祭りハンドブック

神輿の歴史・鑑賞知識から、各地のお祭り情報まで

宮本卯之助◎監修

誠文堂新光社

The Japanese Portable Shrine and Festival Handbook

Their History and Useful Information to Help You Enjoy These Traditional Events

This book covers mikoshi, from the basics, traditional arts and crafts, and history, as well as the introduction of Japan's major festivals.

Supervised by
Miyamoto Unosuke

はじめに

　日本人の心の奥底には、共通の原風景が存在している。それは、四季の移ろいとともに変化する自然の美しさだったり、年ごとに繰り返される地域の行事だったりするが、故郷の記憶とともに深く刻みつけられるものの一つが「祭り」ではないだろうか。

　「祭り」の風景にはいくつもの「絵」がある。町を練り歩く神輿は、一連の「絵」の中の、クライマックスであろう。神社から町へと、神輿は、沿道の人々の視線を一身に集め、掛け声とともににぎやかに、そして、おごそかに進んで行くのである。

　神輿は、神の乗り物である。普段は鎮守の森の深い緑の奥に鎮座する神が、祭りのその時だけ、神輿にお乗りになり、町の隅々を巡り、人々の近くまで降りて来る。

　豪華に、美しく、細部に至るまで心を込めて作られた神の乗り物は、その姿だけで、担ぐ人、見る人の心を動かさずにはおかない。

　江戸時代の町人文化と、明治以降の都市文化の隆盛とともに発達した江戸神輿は、21世紀を迎えた今日にあっても、東京都心や近郊の各地域で、祭のシンボルとして広く認知されている。

　一見したところ、形は神社の小型版ともいうべきものだが、形態を模したという以上に、工芸美術として「神輿」という独自の分野を確立していることは、誰もが認めるところであろう。

　大きく張り出して優美な曲線を描く屋根の造形と、日本伝統の漆塗りで仕上げられた深い光沢。屋根の頂点で雄々しく羽根を広げる鳳凰と、その足元でひときわ輝く屋根紋、そして蕨手。端正にして精緻に仕上げられた堂とその周囲の彫刻群。それらを一つに結び上げる飾り紐。どっしりとして重みのある台輪。

　見れば見るほど、作り手である職人たちの丹誠込めた技に驚嘆せずにはいられない。惜しみなく注がれた伝統技法の数々は、工芸美術の極みにまで達しており、世界に誇る芸術品と言っても過言ではない。

　江戸時代に祭りの中心であった山車に代わって、東京において神輿が重要性を増したのは、明治に入ってからである。街中に電線が張り巡らされ、大きな山車では電線に引っ掛かって支障があるため、高さを気にせずに済む神輿が奨励され、それまでの「宮神輿」に加え「町神輿」が普及したのである。

　太平洋戦争後、急速な経済発展とともに、祭りとその主役である神輿は復活する。近年は、地域のコミュニケーション、世代間の交流のシンボルとしての役割も担い、その必要性を一層増している。

　そして、神輿を大切にし、その技術を後世に伝えていくことは、すぐれた日本の伝統工芸を守ることにつながる点も、忘れてはならないだろう。

　本書では、神輿各部の意匠、製作工程、歴史的な背景までを分かりやすく解説した。日本人が大切にしてきた伝統文化としての神輿を、日本人だけではなく、世界中の人たちがより深く理解できる一助になることを願うものである。

Introduction

In the minds of the Japanese people are some common images arising from childhood memories. Some are the beauty of nature changing with the seasons, while others are scenes of local events which take place every year. I also think the images of matsuri are imprinted in people's mind with the landscape of their hometown. The portrayal of the matsuri is a series of scenes, which culminates with the procession of the mikoshi. From the shrine to the town, the mikoshi makes its way boisterously and ceremoniously with the bearers' energetic shouts, attracting the eyes of the people who fill the streets.

The mikoshi is the carriage of the Shinto god, kami. The kami, normally seated deep in the recesses of the shrine surrounded by wood, comes down to the world of the townspeople in the mikoshi only during the period of the matsuri. That is why the mikoshi is built with heart and soul, and the gorgeous, beautiful and exquisite carriage of the kami captivates the minds of the people.

In the Edo Period (1603 - 1868) the Edo Mikoshi thrived as the ordinary people's culture blossomed in the new capital Edo, present-day Tokyo. It remained a part of people's lives amid the urban development after the Meiji Period (1868 - 1912). Today, in the 21st century, the Edo Mikoshi is recognized as the symbol of the Matsuri in Tokyo and the surrounding areas.

The mikoshi is designed after a shrine, but it is much more than just a miniature shrine. There is no doubt the mikoshi has established an individual art genre. Its roof projects from the body, drawing a graceful curve, with deep luster created by time-tested lacquer work. On top of the roof is the phoenix spreading its wings gallantly, while the crest and warabite shine in gold. Its body is built beautifully and elaborately, adorned by meticulous wood carvings. All the components are kept together by colorful cords, and the whole structure is supported by the robust daiwa. Observing each part carefully, one cannot but be amazed by the craftsmen's outstanding skills. The very best techniques generously applied to the mikoshi are something that Japan can boast to the world.

During the Edo Period, floats called dashi played the major role in the matsuri. It was after the Meiji Period that the mikoshi's importance increased, particularly in Tokyo. As overhead electric cables appeared throughout the town, the mikoshi gradually replaced the lofty dashi. In addition to the shrines' miya-mikoshi, more and more machi-mikoshi, which are mostly owned by neighborhood associations, became common.

After the end of World War 2, Japan made rapid economic growth, and the matsuri and its leading player, the mikoshi, also regained popularity. In recent years the matsuri's significance has been growing as a means of communication within the local communities and between generations.

We also have to keep in mind that Japan's outstanding crafts techniques must be maintained by appreciating the mikoshi and by passing down the mikoshi-building skills for posterity.

This book introduces the components of the mikoshi, how it is built and its historical background. I hope this book will help not only the Japanese, but also people around the world enhance their understanding of the mikoshi, which we have treasured as traditional culture for centuries.

唐破風屋根 白木造り 総彫り 神輿

Karahafu-yane, Shiraki-zukuri (White-wood mikoshi)
Soubori Mikoshi (Sculptured mikoshi)

細部に渡るまで精緻な木彫刻を施した総彫り仕上げの神輿。木目の美しさを生かしている。

Soubori mikoshi. Elaborate carvings are applied on the entire surface, taking advantage of the beauty of the grain.

唐破風屋根の湾曲部分や桝組みの一つひとつに彫刻されている。

Wood carvings are applied on the curved areas of the karahafu-yane and each piece of the masugumi.

屋根の装飾。蕨手には龍が巻きつき繊細な錺金具が施されている。

Roof decorations. The dragons wrap around the warabite with elaborate metal ornaments.

軒下から台輪に至るまでの木彫刻や錺金具は格の高さを演出している。

The sculptures and metal ornaments extending from the eaves all the way down to the daiwa enhance the mikoshi.

唐破風屋根 漆塗り
総彫り 二重台輪 神輿

Mikoshi with Karahafu-yane, Lacquer Coating, Wood Carvings and Double-layered Daiwa

漆塗りの美しさと二重台輪を備えた神輿。屋根には特別注文の大鷲が羽ばたいている。

The mikoshi is marked by the beautiful lacquer-coating and equipped with double-layered daiwa. The bird on the roof is a custom-ordered eagle.

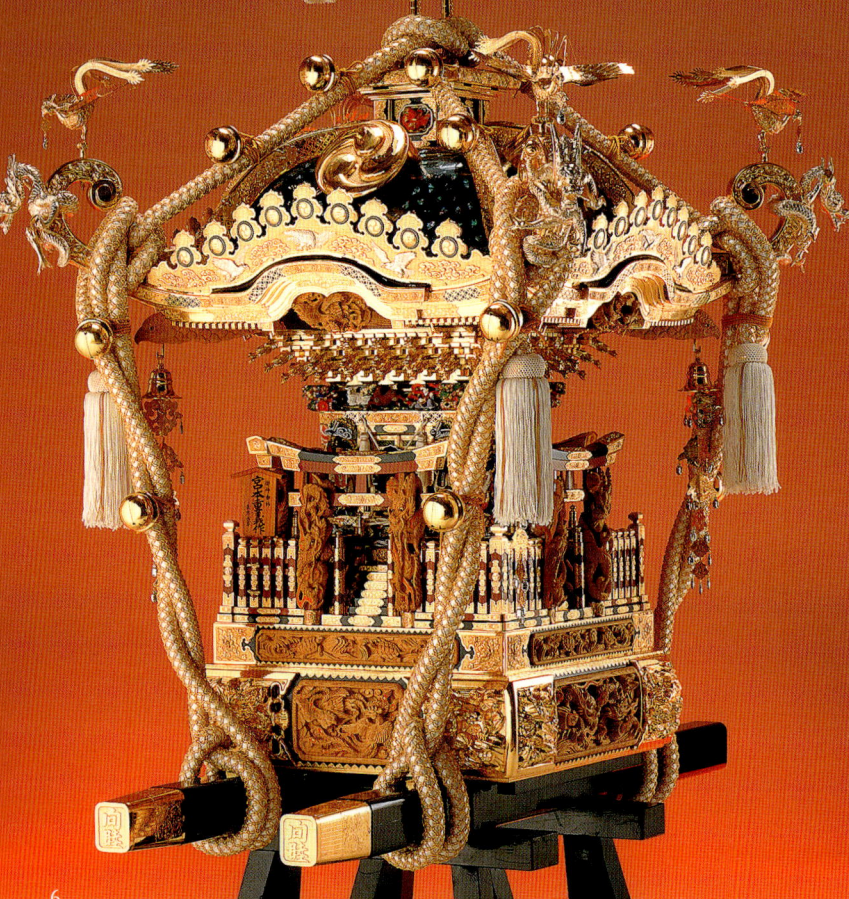

桝組みは金箔押し仕上げで格調の高さと豪華さを兼ね備える。

The masugumi is finished with gold leaf stamping to add to the quality and gorgeousness.

屋根は呂色仕上げの黒に大粒の青貝をはめこんだ螺鈿仕上げ。

The roof is coated with lustrous black lacquer with large inlays of blue seashells.

二重台輪には担ぎ棒を通す棒穴がなく木彫刻のスペースが大きい。

The double-layered daiwa does not have holes for carrying beams, but has ample space for

唐破風屋根
漆塗り 総彫り
神輿

囲垣部分など漆塗りの上に施された錺金具が美しい。木彫刻は繊細さをそのまま生かした白木仕上げ。

The igaki and other parts are coated with lacquer and metal works. The wood carvings take advantage of the texture of uncoated white wood.

Mikoshi with Karahafu-yane, Lacquer Coating and Wood Carvings

三社型神輿
Sanja-Style Mikoshi

屋根の四方で大きくせり上がる蕨手と、ふくらみの少ないすっきりとした形状の屋根が特徴の三社型神輿。

The Sanja-style mikoshi is characterized by the four warabite that curl up high and the sharp outline of the roof.

唐破風屋根
白木造り 神輿

**Shiraki-zukuri Mikoshi
with Karahafu-yane**

屋根の中央部に湾曲がある唐破風屋根の神輿。木彫刻に彩色をしない上品な白木仕上げ。

The karahafu roof is marked by the eaves elevated in the middle. It is a classic white-wood mikoshi with no color-coating on the sculptures.

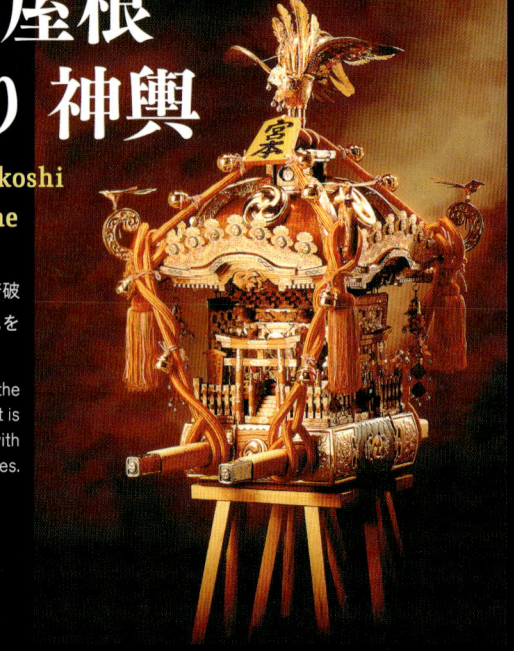

唐破風屋根
漆塗り 神輿

**Lacquer-coated Mikoshi
with Karahafu-yane**

金と黒、飾り紐(かざりひも)の紫の3色を基調にした落ちついた雰囲気の漆塗り神輿。

Quiet-toned lacquered mikoshi, using gold, black, and purple of the kazarihimo as the base colors.

延屋根
のべやね
白木造り 神輿

Shiraki-zukuri Mikoshi with Nobe-yane

のきつら
軒面の緩やかなカーブに並ぶ吹き返しが美しい延屋根の神輿。

The fukikaeshi adorns the gently curved eaves of the nobe roof.

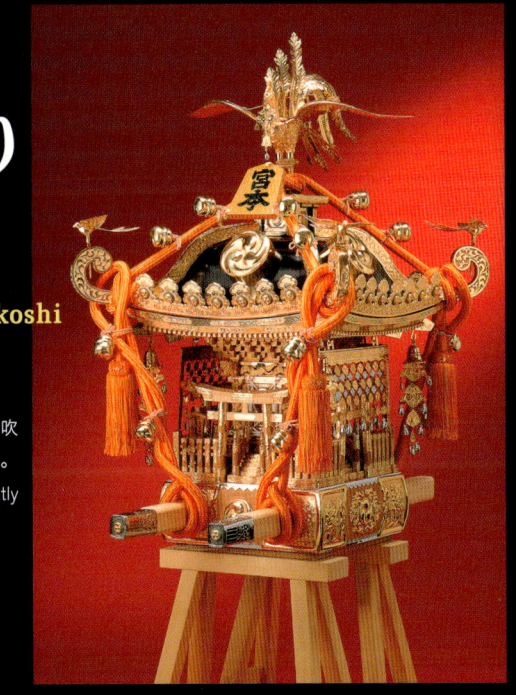

延屋根
漆塗り 神輿

Lacquer-coated Mikoshi with Nobe-yane

全体が直線的なフォルムで台輪もふくらみの少ない形になっている。

A mikoshi with a sharp silhouette. The surface of the daiwa is almost straight.

【目次】
Contents

はじめに……2
Introduction

口絵……4
Frontispieces

参考文献・監修者紹介……143
References, about the editorial supervisor

第1章 神輿を飾る意匠を見る……15
Chapter 1　Appreciating the design of the mikoshi

神輿を形づくる各部分の名称……16
Names of the mikoshi components

神輿の印象を決める屋根の代表的な形状……18
Typical shape of the roof
that determines the mikoshi's impression

権威と華やかさを際立たせる翼……20
Phoenix wings accentuate
a mikoshi's stateliness and opulence

祭神を表す神紋と鳳凰を支える台座……22
Shinmon represents the enshrined kami,
while daiza support the houou

屋根の曲線美を強調する装飾……24
Ornaments that emphasize
the roof's graceful curved lines

所属を表す札と錺金具で際立つ屋根の装飾……26
Name plates and metal ornaments
on the roof

「輿」から受け継がれた造形……28
The design modeled after the palanquin

精密な構造からなる木地組み……30
Woodwork with its intricate structure

神社建築にならった神の居場所……32
The space for the kami is a miniature shrine

縁起物に工夫を凝らして飾りつけ……34
Lucky objects lend enhancement
to the mikoshi

神聖な領域・堂を取り囲む装飾物……36
Adornments for the sacred area

神輿の装飾で唯一の繊維製部分……38
The only fibrous product on a mikoshi

神輿を頑強に支える鮮やかな土台……40
The lavish base provides
a solid foundation for the mikoshi

錺金具で彩られる台輪の装飾……42
Ornamental pieces that embellish daiwa

木彫刻でより引き立つ台輪の装飾……44
Wooden carvings add to
the aesthetic appeal of the daiwa

第2章 神輿製作の職人技を知る……47
Chapter 2 Learning the techniques of mikoshi construction

神輿は職人技の粋の結晶 …… 48
The mikoshi is the
crystallization of artisanship

木地部製作のための木工工具 …… 50
Wood processing tools

神輿に適した木材の選定 …… 52
Choosing the appropriate wood

社寺建築も神輿製作も図面は原寸で描かれる 54
Full-sized drawings are used in
building a temple, shrine or mikoshi

重量と衝撃に耐える堅固な台輪 …… 55
Solid daiwa endure weight and shock

神輿の壮麗な屋根を支える骨組み …… 56
Framework to support
the mikoshi's enormous roof

屋根の形状を決定づける野地板張り …… 58
Nojiita-bari determines
the shape of the roof

装飾と機能性を兼ね備える桝組み …… 60
Masugumi serves
decorative and functional purposes

木地師の確かな仕事が骨格を作る …… 62
Kiji-shi's mastery
completes the framework

鋳物によって作られる鳳凰と蕨手 …… 64
Houou and warabite
made by metal casting

漆だけが持つ特性を生かす工具類 …… 66
Tools maximize lacquer's characteristics

漆塗りの基礎となる下地作業 …… 68
Foundation coating for lacquer work

下塗り・中塗りをていねいに …… 70
No pains spared in applying
the base and middle coatings

漆塗りの最終工程上塗り・仕上げ塗り …… 72
Final coating completes the lacquering

神輿を絢爛豪華に彩る金箔 …… 74
Gold leaf adds to the mikoshi's splendor

技の数だけ存在する木彫刻工具 …… 76
As many carving tools as
the number of techniques

木彫刻で神輿が生きた造形に …… 78
Wood carving gives life to the mikoshi

錺職人の伝統技法を支える工具 …… 80
Tools support traditional metal chasing
techniques

錺金具が神輿を豪華に荘厳に …… 82
Metal ornaments adds glitz and
grandeur to the mikoshi

伝統の彩色技法で神輿を鮮やかに …… 84
Time-honored technique
makes the mikoshi colorful

伝統技術が一つにまとまる組み立て …… 85
Combining traditional techniques
into one mikoshi

江戸神輿の「粋」と「いなせ」を守る神輿師 86
The bearer of the spirit and
style of mikoshi

第3章 伝統の神輿を担ぐ……87
Chapter 3 Carrying the traditional mikoshi

神輿の大きさと担ぐ人数 …… 88
The size of the mikoshi and
the number of bearers

飾り紐の掛け方 …… 90
The kazarihimo is more than
just an ornament

担ぎ棒の組み方 …… 92
How the carrying beams are assembled

祭りをにぎやかにする山車 …… 94
Dashi adds to a matsuri's festivity

祭礼での神輿の準備 …… 96
Preparing the mikoshi for the ritual

神輿のじょうずな担ぎ方 …… 98
How to carry a mikoshi

神輿を保管する方法 …… 99
How to keep the mikoshi in good shape

古くなった神輿は修理して長く使う …… 100
Repair and maintenance
for the longevity of the mikoshi

第4章 神輿と祭りの歴史を探る ……… 101
Chapter 4 Learning the history of mikoshi and matsuri

日本の祭りの起源と人々の祈り ……… 102
The origin of matsuri and
the people's prayers

神輿の原型である神社の建築様式 ……… 106
The shrine architecture as
the original model of the mikoshi

輿という乗り物と神輿の起源 ……… 110
Koshi and the origin of mikoshi

江戸時代の庶民の気質と祭り ……… 112
The spirit of the ordinary people
in the Edo Period and the matsuri

現代に受け継がれる祭りと神輿 ……… 114
Legacy of the matsuri and the mikoshi

神輿作りの伝統技術と変遷 ……… 118
Traditional mikoshi-building
techniques and traditions

今こそ日本中で祭りを ……… 120
Promoting the matsuri nationwide

第5章 全国の祭りを旅する ……… 121
Chapter 5 Exploring Japan's regional matsuri

青森ねぶた祭 青森県青森市 ……… 122
Aomori Nebuta Matsuri (Aomori City, Aomori)

弘前ねぷたまつり 青森県弘前市 ……… 123
Hirosaki Neputa Matsuri (Hirosaki City, Aomori)

角館のお祭り 秋田県仙北市 ……… 124
The Festival of Kakunodate (Senboku City, Akita)

仙台・青葉まつり 宮城県仙台市 ……… 125
Sendai Aoba Matsuri (Sendai City, Miyagi)

二本松ちょうちん祭り 福島県二本松市 ……… 126
Nihonmatsu Chochin Matsuri
(Nihonmatsu City, Fukushima)

秩父神社例大祭 埼玉県秩父市 ……… 127
Chichibu Shrine Annual Festival
(Chichibu City, Saitama)

八坂祭典熊谷うちわ祭 埼玉県熊谷市 ……… 128
Yasaka Saiten Kumagaya Uchiwa Matsuri
(Kumagaya City, Saitama)

桐生八木節まつり 群馬県桐生市 ……… 129
Kiryu Yagibushi Matsuri (Kiryu City, Gunma)

三社祭 東京都台東区 ……… 130
Sanja Matsuri (Taito Ward, Tokyo)

山王祭 東京都千代田区 ……… 131
Sanoh Matsuri (Chiyoda Ward, Tokyo)

富岡八幡宮例祭 東京都江東区 ……… 132
Tomioka Hachimangu Reisai (Koto Ward, Tokyo)

神田祭 東京都千代田区 ……… 133
Kanda Matsuri (Chiyoda Ward, Tokyo)

茅ヶ崎海岸浜降祭 神奈川県茅ヶ崎市 ……… 134
Chigasaki Kaigan Hamaorisai
(Chigasaki City, Kanagawa)

高岡御車山祭 富山県高岡市 ……… 135
Takaoka Mikurumayama Matsuri
(Takaoka City, Toyama)

浜松まつり 静岡県浜松市 ……… 136
Hamamatsu Matsuri (Hamamatsu City, Shizuoka)

京都祇園祭 京都府京都市 ……… 137
Kyoto Gion Matsuri (Kyoto City, Kyoto)

天神祭 大阪府大阪市 ……… 138
Tenjin Matsuri (Osaka City, Osaka)

西条まつり 愛媛県西条市 ……… 139
Saijo Matsuri (Saijo City, Ehime)

日田祇園祭 大分県日田市 ……… 140
Hita Gion Matsuri (Hita City, Oita)

伊万里トンテントン祭り 佐賀県伊万里市 ……… 141
Imari Tontenton Matsuri (Imari City, Saga)

那覇大綱挽まつり 沖縄県那覇市 ……… 142
Naha Otsunahiki Matsuri (Naha City, Okinawa)

第1章
Chapter 1

神輿を飾る意匠を見る

Appreciating the Design of the Mikoshi

神輿には外側だけでも名称のある部位が
40以上あり、社寺建築などに見られる
伝統的な意匠が凝らしてある。
神輿を飾る豪華で繊細な意匠を見る。

The mikoshi consists of numerous parts—more than forty distinct components on the outer side alone—which are designed in the same way as traditional temples and shrines. In this chapter, we take a look at the designs of the mikoshi, which are both magnificent and delicate.

神輿を形づくる各部分の名称

Components of the Mikoshi

神が本来祭られている神社を模して造られる神輿は、屋根・堂・台輪の3つの部分から成る。

Modeled after a Shinto shrine, where the kami (god) is housed, the mikoshi, is composed of three main parts: the roof, the body, and the base.

神はふだんは神社に祀られている。人々は自ら神社に足を運びお参りをすることで、神と対面する。しかし祭りのときなどには神輿に神が移されて町中をくまなく巡る（巡行する＝渡御ともいう）。輿はもともと、貴人の乗り物のことであった。神輿とは神が乗る輿なのである。

　神輿は大きく分けて3つの部分から成る、第1は遠くからも見える屋根。第2は鳥居や囲垣など実際の神社と同様の構造を備えた堂。第3はこれらを載せ担ぎ棒を通す台輪である。それらのどの部分にも伝統と格式を現代に伝える職人芸の粋が施されている。

Normally, the kami is believed to reside within a Shinto shrine, where people visit to pay their respects. During a festival, however, the kami is temporarily moved into the mikoshi, a portable shrine, which is then paraded around the town. Koshi means a traditional palanquin used to carry noble people in olden times, whereas mikoshi serves to transport kami exclusively.

The mikoshi is roughly composed of three sections: the roof, which is conspicuous even from afar, the dou (body), built in the same structure as a shrine, including the torii (gate) and igaki (fence), and the daiwa, through which the timber shafts to carry the mikoshi are placed. Every inch of these components is gorgeously decorated by skilled craftsmen, who carry on the ancient traditions and formalities to this day.

- ❶ 鳳凰（大鳥ともいう） Houou / Ohtori
- ❷ 露盤 Roban
- ❸ 吹き返し巴 Fukikaei-tomoe
- ❹ 屋根紋 Yanemon
- ❺ 野筋 Nosuji
- ❻ 蕨手 Warabite
- ❼ 吹き返し Fukikaeshi
- ❽ 駒札 Komafuda
- ❾ 小鳥（燕ともいう） Kotori / Tsubame
- ❿ 軒面 Nokitsura
- ⓫ 隅木 Sumiki
- ⓬ 垂木 Taruki
- ⓭ 飾り紐 Kazarihimo
- ⓮ 鈴 Suzu
- ⓯ 紐房 Himofusa
- ⓰ 桝組み Masugumi
- ⓱ 瓔珞 Youraku
- ⓲ 風鐸（風鈴ともいう） Fuuchaku / Fuurin
- ⓳ 銀杏 Ichou
- ⓴ 狛犬 Komainu
- ㉑ 長押 Nageshi
- ㉒ 唐戸 Karato
- ㉓ 堂柱 Doubashira
- ㉔ 鏡 Kagami
- ㉕ 鳥居 Torii
- ㉖ 作人札 Sakuninfuda
- ㉗ 擬宝珠 Giboshi
- ㉘ 勾欄 Kouran
- ㉙ 囲垣 Igaki
- ㉚ 腰桝 Koshimasu
- ㉛ 地福 Jifuku
- ㉜ 階 Kizahashi
- ㉝ 棒穴 Bouana
- ㉞ 台輪隅金物 Daiwasumi-kanamono
- ㉟ 棒先金物 Bousaki-kanamono
- ㊱ 台輪紋 Daiwamon
- ㊲ 剃刀 Kamisori
- ㊳ 覆輪 Fukurin
- ㊴ 泥摺り Dorosuri

Chapter 1: Appreciating the Design of the Mikoshi 17

神輿の印象を決める屋根の代表的な形状

Typical shape of the roof that determines the mikoshi's impression

唐破風屋根・延屋根
<small>からはふやね のべやね</small>

Karahafu-yane, Nobe-yane

曲線が重厚感と華やかさを感じさせる唐破風屋根と、
直線的な軒面に屋根紋が映える延屋根。

A karahafu roof's curvy lines represent massiveness and magnificence, whereas the crest stands out on the straight line of a nobe roof.

軒面の中央部が湾曲していて重厚感と威厳に満ちた唐破風屋根。
Karahafu roof's curved eaves give a majestic, dignified atmosphere.

神輿の形状はその神輿が所属する神社の社殿の形状にならうことがほとんどで、屋根も神社の形状と同じにすることが多い。神輿の屋根には大きく分けて2種類ある。1つは中央部が大きく湾曲している唐破風型の屋根で、平安時代から始まったとされるこの形は寺院や城にも見られる。もう1つは軒面に湾曲のない延屋根である。近年の延屋根は四方に向かってせり上がるラインを描くものが多い。三社型の延屋根はより直線に近い。

In most cases a mikoshi is modeled after the structure of the shrine it came from, and therefore, the roof is usually designed the same way as that of the shrine. There are two major types of mikoshi roofs: karahafu style and nobe style. The karahafu roof features eaves which are elevated in the middle. The karahafu roof is said to have first appeared in the Heian Period (794-1192) and has been used in many temples and castles. The other type is the nobe roof, with straight eaves. In recent years nobe roofs with upswept ends have become popular, while traditional Sanja-style nobe roof are almost straight.

軒面に湾曲のない延屋根。四方に向かって少し反り返っている。

Nobe roof's eaves are straight with slightly upswept edges.

三社型神輿の屋根はより直線的な延屋根を持っている。

Traditional Sanja-style roof has almost straight lower edges

Chapter 1: Appreciating the Design of the Mikoshi

権威と華やかさを際立たせる翼

Phoenix wings accentuate the mikoshi's stateliness and opulence

鳳凰・小鳥
(ほうおう・ことり)

Houou (Chinese phoenix), Kotori (little bird)

帝の乗り物である「鳳輦」にもついていたとされる鳳凰。
翼を広げて神輿の到来を人々に知らせる。

The houou is said to have graced emperors' palanquins.
It spreads its wings to signal the arrival of the mikoshi.

神輿の一番上で羽根を広げる鳳凰。
Houou spreading its wings on top of a mikoshilower edges.

四隅の蕨手の上に据えられた小鳥。
Kotori perched on the warabite at the roof's four corners.

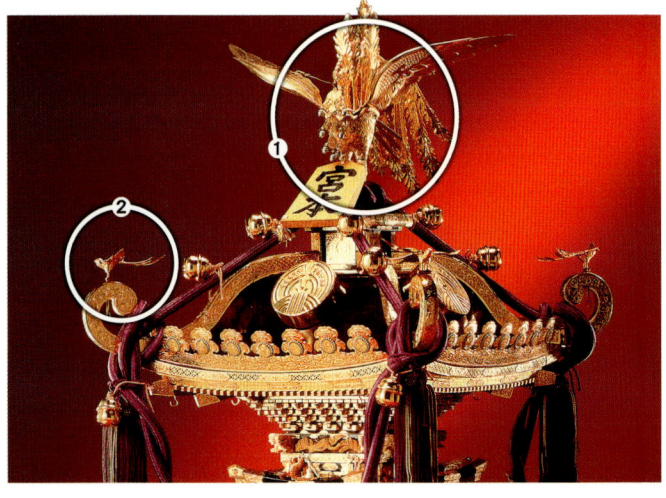

神輿の屋根には頂点に鳳凰（大鳥ともいう）が載って翼を広げている。鳳凰は伝説上の霊的な動物で、帝の象徴にもなっていたとされ、また、寺院の装飾としても登場する。神輿の頂きにある鳳凰は、体は鋳物で作られ、羽根部分などの装飾を錺金具で仕上げる。4か所の蕨手の上には小鳥（燕ともいう）が、神輿の中心に尾を向けて、外側に頭が来るように載せられている。

On the peak of the mikoshi's roof perches the houou, also called ohtori (great bird), with its wings spread wide. A spiritual creature in legends, houou have often been used as a symbol of the emperor and also as a popular motif of temple decorations. The body of the houou on the mikoshi is made of cast metal, and decorative pieces are attached onto the wings. Also on the warabite at the roof's four corners are kotori (little birds), sometimes called tsubame (swallows), with their tails directed toward the center of the mikoshi and their heads pointed outward.

神社の祭神によっては、このような鷲が載っている神輿もある。

An eagle is in the place of the houou, indicating that the bird is associated with a shrine.

一般的な形をした鳳凰。

A common type of houou.

小さいながら存在感のある小鳥。

A small yet imposing kotori.

Chapter 1: Appreciating the Design of the Mikoshi

祭神を表す神紋と鳳凰を支える台座

Shinmon (shrine crest) represents the enshrined kami, while daiza supports the houou

屋根紋・露盤

Yanemon, Roban

鳳凰を支える土台が露盤。屋根紋は屋根の4面に取りつけられ、神輿の出自を周囲に示す。

Roban serves as the base for the houou.
The yanemon is attached to the four roof plates to signal the mikoshi's origin.

鳳凰や駒札が取り付けられた露盤。
The roban holds the houou and komafuda.

屋根紋は多くの場合、神輿が所属する神社の紋から取る。

In many cases the crest of the shrine the mikoshi is associated with is used as the yanemon.

屋根の頂上で鳳凰や駒札を据えつける箱状のものを露盤と呼ぶ。露盤は日本の社寺建築に欠かせないもので、塔の屋根の頭頂部を押さえて飾りを載せる土台になる部分である。神輿の屋根の４面には紋章が輝いている。この紋は神輿が所属する神社の神紋から取っている場合が多く、ほかにも菊などの花をモチーフにしたものや、神輿を所有する町内会の独自の図案を紋として採用することもある。屋根紋の中でも多くみられるのが巴紋である。

The small box on which the houou and komafuda are attached is the roban. An indispensable part of the structures of Japanese temples and shrines, the roban is placed on the mikoshi's roof to serve as the base for ornaments. Meanwhile, on the four sides of the roof are crests. In general, the crest of the shrine with which the mikoshi is associated is used. Some mikoshi display a crest of the chrysanthemum flower, while others use an original design by the neighborhood association connected with the shrine. Among the most popular designs for the yanemon is the tomoe crest.

稲荷神社の神輿はこのような稲穂を紋にすることがある。屋根紋が３つ、５つなど奇数で複数のものもある。

Inari Shrines, dedicated to the deity of agriculture, often use rice stalks as the motif of the crest. Some mikoshi have odd numbers (usually three or five) of yanemon.

鳳凰ではなく擬宝珠が載せられた露盤。

This roban is topped with giboshi (onion-shaped ornament) instead of houou.

Chapter 1: Appreciating the Design of the Mikoshi

屋根の曲線美を強調する装飾

Ornaments that emphasize the roof's graceful curved lines

野筋・蕨手
(のすじ・わらびて)

Nosuji, Warabite

屋根の4面の合わせ目を飾る野筋。
野筋の先にある蕨手は装飾と同時に構造上の役割もある。

The nosuji adorn the joint lines of the four roof plates.
The warabite is attached to the lower end of the nosuji,
to serve both decorative and structural purposes.

屋根の四隅の曲線を走る野筋。

Nosuji run down along the roof's four curves.

植物のワラビのように巻いた蕨手。

Warabite curl up like the warabi fern (bracken fiddleheads).

神輿の屋根は、六角や八角といった特殊な形状のものを除いて、通常4つの面から構成される。その4面の板と板が合わさる部分を曲線に合わせて縦方向に押さえるのが野筋である。野筋本体は木製で漆が塗られ錺金具が取りつけられる。金具は下の漆の美しさを生かして透かしが入っているものがある。4か所の野筋の先にある蕨手は鋳物で作られているものが多く、その上に錺金具の飾りがつくこともある。蕨手に巻きつけられた飾り紐は、神輿全体を引き締め強度を増す役割も持っている。

Although there are some hexagonal or octagonal mikoshi, most mikoshi are square-shaped. Nosuji is the bar placed along the curved line where two roof plates meet. The wooden nosuji is lacquer-coated and covered with a metal layer, often with openwork through which beautiful lacquer underneath can be seen. Warabite is the part attached at the lower end of the nosuji. Usually, warabite are made of cast metal and decorated with metal ornaments. The brightly-colored cords looped around the warabite tie the mikoshi components together and increase its sturdiness.

銀メッキの龍が巻きついた豪華な蕨手。

A decorative warabite with a silver-plated dragon coiling around itad of houou.

三社型神輿の蕨手は通常のものよりも内側に巻き上がっている。

The warabite of the Sanja-style mikoshi curl tighter than normal ones.

錺金具を施した蕨手は下の黒漆が透けて見える。

Black lacquer coating on the warabite can be seen through the openwork

Chapter 1: Appreciating the Design of the Mikoshi

所属を表す札と錺金具で際立つ屋根の装飾

The komafuda indicates the mikoshi's affiliation, with the metal ornaments adding to the flamboyance of the roof

駒札・吹き返し・隅木　*Komafuda, Fukikaeshi, Ssumiki*

駒札にはその神輿が所属するものの名称が掲げられる。
屋根を飾る吹き返しは実用の意味もある。

Komafuda, which identifies who owns the mikoshi,
and fukikaeshi, which serves for decorative and practical purposes

屋根の縁を飾る吹き返し。
Fukikaeshi adorn the fringes of the roof.

神輿の所属を表す駒札。
Komafuda signals who owns the mikoshi.

将棋の駒の形をした木の板が駒札である。神輿は、神社に所属するほか町会ごとに持っているケースも多く、その神輿がどこに所属するのかを識別するためにつけられている。屋根の縁に沿って並んでいるのが吹き返しで、一つひとつに屋根紋と同じ紋が刻されている。昔は神輿の屋根に向けて賽銭が投げられることがあり、その硬貨を受け止める役割もあったといわれている。蕨手の根元にある隅木にも装飾が施される。

The wooden plate shaped like a Japanese chess piece is called the komafuda. In most cases, a mikoshi is owned by a shrine or a neighborhood association. If you look at the komafuda, you will know who the mikoshi belongs to. The fukikaeshi is the ornament attached to the lower edge of the roof. The same crest as the yanemon is carved on each small plate of the fukikaeshi. In olden times, people would toss offertory coins at mikoshi, and the fukikaeshi was useful in catching the money. The sumiki is the piece attached under the warabite, and is also beautifully decorated.

吹き返しは一つひとつの円の中に屋根紋と同じ紋が打ち出されている。

Each plate of the fukikaeshi is carved with the yanemon crestdleheads).

白木のまま龍の彫刻が施された隅木。

Sumiki with dragon carving on bare wood.

Chapter 1: Appreciating the Design of the Mikoshi

「輿」から
受け継がれた造形
The design modeled after the palanquin

瓔珞・風鐸
Youraku, Fuchaku

尊い存在は御簾の向こうに存在を感じるものである。
繊細な装飾が神輿の神秘性を増す。

Divine presence is to be felt through a screen.
The delicate decoration adds to the mikoshi's sacred aura.

堂の四方に掛かっている瓔珞。

Youraku shields the dou on each of the four sides.

屋根の四隅に提げられる風鐸。

Fuchaku hang from the four corners of the roof.

神輿には随所に職人技が尽くされるが、瓔珞はそれを見えないように隠してしまう。古来、恐れ多いものはじかに見ることはせず、御簾などを通して隙間からその姿を垣間みるものである。瓔珞は神輿に乗る神に対しての御簾の役割を果たす。ただ、神輿が町を練り歩く際には傷まないよう取り外すことも多い。風鐸は、寺院などの建物の四隅にあるものを模している。風鐸も担ぐ際には外されることが多い。

Craftsmen's skills are demonstrated exhaustively in every piece of the mikoshi, but as a matter of fact, many of them are hidden behind the youraku. Since ancient times, an object of worship was not supposed to be directly looked upon, but to be felt through a misu screen. Youraku serves the same purpose as misu, hiding the kami resting within the mikoshi. When the mikoshi is carried around the town, however, the youraku is often removed to prevent damage. The fuchaku are modeled after the bells hanging at the four corners of temples or other traditional structures. Oftentimes the fuchaku is also taken off during processions of the mikoshi.

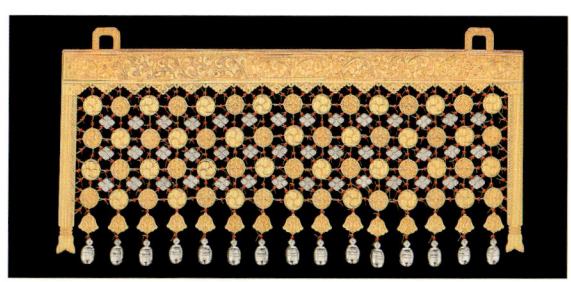

金の三つ巴と菱を挟んで組み合わされた瓔珞。

Youraku designed with gold mitsudomoe (triplicate tomoe) and lozenge motifs.

風鐸は瓔珞とのバランスも考えたデザインである。
Fuchaku is designed to fit in with the youraku.

四角いメタルを連ねて作られた珍しいデザインの瓔珞。
An unusual youraku with strings of square metal pieces.

Chapter 1: Appreciating the Design of the Mikoshi

精密な構造からなる木組み

Woodwork with an intricate structure

桝組みますぐみ *Masugumi*

細い堂に載った壮麗な屋根の重みを分散して支える桝組みは、機能と美しさを同時に叶える。

Exquisite work of art to distribute the weight of the massive roof onto the smaller dou.

機能と美しさをあわせ持つ桝組み。

Masugumi has both functional and aesthetic values.

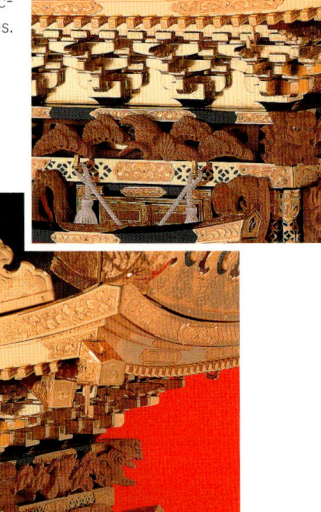

桝組みは、古くから日本建築の屋根の重量を支える構造として存在していたものだ。全体は大きな四角錐を逆さまにした形の構造物で、細長い角材である肘木が縦横に交差し、桝と呼ばれる小さな四角い木の部品に載っており、この肘木と桝のいくつもの複雑な組み合わせが桝組みである。桝組みは何段か重なり、下にいくほどすぼむ形になっている。桝組みには金箔押しや彫刻を施すなど、さらに装飾が加えられることも少なくない。

Masugumi, shaped like a pyramid turned upside down, is a time-honored architectural method that has been used to support the hefty roof of traditional Japanese structures. A grid of thin square timbers is placed on a layer of wooden cubes called masu, which refers to the wooden square cups for drinking sake. Masugumi is a multi-tiered structure with a layer on top of another, smaller layer. In many cases the timbers and cubes are gilded or sculptured.

白木を生かした木彫で豪華に飾られた桝組み。

Masugumi with gorgeous carving making use of the wood texture.

一般的な形の桝組み。
下の段にいくほどすぼまる。

Typically, the masugumi narrows down toward the bottom.

全体に金箔押しを施した豪華な仕上げの桝組み。

Flamboyant gilding is applied all over the masugumi.

Chapter 1: Appreciating the Design of the Mikoshi

神社建築にならった神の居場所

The space for the kami is a miniature shrine

堂 どう

Dou (the body)

所属する神社の構造を再現して造られることが多く、
本殿（ほんでん）と周囲を構成する要素が凝縮される。

A mikoshi is built in the same way as the shrine it belongs to,
with the elements of the main hall and other objects packed into the dou.

神社のあらゆる要素を精巧な細工で表現している堂。

The wooden areas are lacquered and covered with metal ornaments.

木地部分に漆を塗り、その上に錺金具がはめ込まれている。

Uncoated wooden dou with sculptures on the entire surface. Dragons wrap around the gate pillars.

神輿は神の御霊を神社の本殿から迎える場所である。そのため神社の構造を細部に至るまで再現して造られる。特に堂は、神社そのもののミニチュアとでもいうべき構造になっており、唐戸、匂欄など神社の本殿部分と、鳥居、囲垣など境内の建造物も含め全体として神社の境内をイメージしたものになっている。そして、それらすべてに、木彫刻、極彩色、錺金具などの緻密な装飾が施されている。

As temporary accommodation for the kami residing within the shrine's main hall, the mikoshi is a detailed reproduction of the shrine. Especially, the dou is considered a miniature shrine, which includes the fixtures of the main hall, such as karato doors and koran (parapet), as well as torii (gate) and igaki (fence) which are found in the precincts. All the components are elaborately carved, brightly painted, or decorated with metal ornaments.

白木造りで総彫りの神輿の堂。鳥居には龍が巻きついている。

Uncoated wooden dou with sculptures on the entire surface. Dragons wrap around the gate pillars.

堂の周囲に匂欄がない、比較的シンプルな作りの漆塗り神輿。

Lacquered mikoshi in a relatively simple structure with no koran around the dou.

Chapter 1: Appreciating the Design of the Mikoshi

縁起物に工夫を凝らして飾りつけ

Lucky objects lend enhancement to the mikoshi

狛犬・唐戸・鏡

Komainu, Karato, Kagami

神社にふさわしい縁起物の数々が、
職人技の粋を集めてふんだんに盛り込まれる。

Profuse decoration with auspicious objects created with painstaking craftsmanship.

四隅に1対ずつ8体の狛犬。
A pair of komainu sitting on each side, eight in total.

漆塗りと錺金具で装飾された唐戸。
Lacquered karato embellished with metal ornaments.

唐戸の脇を守る右大臣と左大臣の像。
Statues of Udaijin (Minister of the Right) and Sadaijin (Minister of the Left) by the karato.

神社を訪れると参道の両側に1対の狛犬が置かれている。もともとはインドのライオンを模したものだといわれており、日本には霊的な存在として伝わった。神輿の狛犬は桝組みの下に取りつけられており、四隅に1対ずつ計8体取りつけられているものもある。神社から神の御霊を迎えて神輿の本殿に入れる扉が唐戸である。唐戸の前面にはご神体である鏡が掛けられているが、神社では本殿の中にある。唐戸の周囲にも精緻な装飾が施されている。

At a shrine, a pair of komainu (guardian dogs) is found on either side of the approach leading to the main hall. Originally created after lions in India, they were introduced in Japan as spiritual creatures. The mikoshi is also guarded by komainu, sitting under the masugumi. In some cases, you will see one pair at each corner, eight in total. When the soul of the kami is moved from the shrine to the mikoshi, it enters through the karato door. In front of the karato is a kagami (mirror), an article considered a sacred body of the kami, although in a shrine, kagami are normally housed in the main hall. The karato is also fringed with lavish decoration.

唐戸の上から紐で掛けられている鏡。

Kagami is hung over the karato with strings.

桝組みの下にある極彩色が施された狛犬。

Brightly colored komainu under the masugumi.

Chapter 1: Appreciating the Design of the Mikoshi

神聖な領域・堂を
取り囲む装飾物

Adornments for the sacred area

囲垣・鳥居・階・作人札 *Igaki, Torii, Kizahashi, Sakuninfuda*

神域と俗世を隔てる囲垣と鳥居は神社そのままに作られる。
作人札は神輿師の気概と誇りを表す。

Igaki and torii indicate the boundary between the sacred area
and the mundane world just as in the shrine,
while the sakuninfuda represents the mikoshi builders' spirit and pride.

① 神輿師の名を記した作人札。
Sakuninfuda, a name place of the chief mikoshi builder.

② 鳥居とその向こうに続く階。
Beyond the torii stretches the kizahashi.

36 　第1章：神輿を飾る意匠を見る

神聖な場所である神社は石の垣根で囲まれ出入り口には鳥居が建ち、俗世と隔てられている。神輿にはそれらを模した囲垣と鳥居が小さいながらも威厳を持って据えられている。神社の本殿に昇る階段は階という古い名前で呼ばれ、これは神輿においても同様である。作人札は、神輿製作を統括する神輿師の名前が書かれた木の札で、これが掲げられているのは、神輿師をはじめとした全職人の誇りの表明だともいえる。

A shrine is a sacred place separated from the outside world by stone fences and torii gates. The mikoshi is also equipped with small but solemn igaki and torii. The steps leading to a shrine's main hall as well as those in mikoshi are called kizahashi, an old Japanese term for stairs. Sakuninfuda is the wooden plate indicating the name of the chief builder who led the construction of the mikoshi. The plate represents the pride of not only the chief builder, but also all the craftsmen engaged.

作人札も漆塗りで仕上げた最高級品。
Finished with lacquer work, the sakuninfuda itself is a top-notch art object.

鳥居や囲垣の錺金具には屋根紋と同じ紋章が刻まれ、鳥居には龍が巻きついている。
The ornaments on torii and igaki are marked with the same crest as the yanemon. Dragons are coiling around the torii's pillars.

漆塗りの鳥居や囲垣に施された錺金具が輝く。
Adornments glitter on the lacquered torii and igaki.

神輿の装飾で
唯一の繊維製部分

The only fibrous product on a mikoshi

飾り紐
<small>かざ　ひも</small>

Kazarihimo

魔除けの鈴が結ばれ房が垂れる飾り紐は、神輿にしなやかな美しさを加える。

Kazarihimo, with a bell to ward off evil,
and a tassel adds graceful charm to the mikoshi.

飾り紐の上部は蕨手に巻きつけられる。
The upper part of the kazarihimo is wrapped around the warabite.

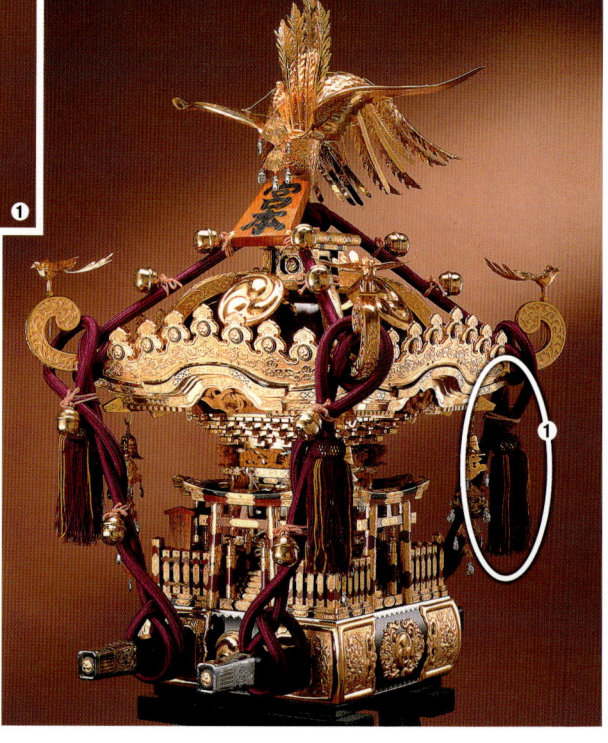

神輿が持つ木地の質感の堅牢さや錺金具のきらびやかさに対して、飾り紐は唯一の繊維製部分であり、しなやかな美しさを装飾に加えている。紐の色には赤、青、金茶、紫などがあるが、その色は神輿の仕上げ方によって選ばれる。黒漆で仕上げた神輿には紫が映え、白木を生かした神輿には明るい金茶を合わせることが多い。紐のところどころに掛けられる鈴は、涼やかな音が神を喜ばせるとも、魔除けになるともされる。

The only fibrous component of mikoshi, elegant kazarihimo makes a clear contrast to the wooden components' sturdiness or metal ornaments' glamor. The color of the cord ranges from red, blue, golden brown to purple, and is chosen according to the mikoshi's type. A black-lacquered mikoshi looks brilliant with purple cords, while a bright gold-brown cord is often paired with a mikoshi made of uncoated wood. The bells tied to the cord are said to please the kami with their cool sound, and also to dispel evil.

水あさぎ色の網掛け飾り紐。
Netted pale blue kazarihimo.

高貴な印象の紫の紐が
黒漆の塗り神輿に映える。
Purple, considered a noble color, stands out against black lacquer.

明るく輝く金茶の飾り紐は
白木造りの神輿に合う。
The bright golden cord and wooden mikoshi go well together.

Chapter 1: Appreciating the Design of the Mikoshi

神輿を頑強に支える
鮮やかな土台

The lavish base provides a solid foundation for the mikoshi.

台輪(だいわ) *Daiwa*

激しい衝撃にも耐える伝統の組み木製法を駆使して作られ堂と屋根を受け止める。

Built with the traditional kumiki method,
the base supports the massive roof and body which are moved wildly.

ふんだんに木彫刻を施しその周囲を錺金具で彩った台輪。
通常の台輪の上にもう一段台輪を設けた二重台輪で棒穴のないタイプ。

Daiwa sumptuously sculptured and covered with metal ornaments.
This is a double-layered type with no beam holes.

神輿は大きいものだと重量が500kgを超えることも珍しくなく、それが担ぎ手によって上下左右に激しく揺さぶられる。この神輿が百年、二百年と受け継がれるほど長持ちするのは、主要部分に金属のくぎを使わない伝統の組み木製法によって作られているからだ。木と木が接する面にわずかな隙間（遊び）が生まれ衝撃を吸収する。そしてもちろん台輪にも木彫刻や錺金具による装飾が施される。台輪が2段になった二重台輪の豪華な神輿もある。

It is not uncommon that the mikoshi weighs more than 500 kg and is shaken up and down, left and right during the procession. But some mikoshi have been handled this way for over 100 or even 200 years, a testament to the traditional kumiki methods used in the important parts. Since the method does not involve metal nails, the narrow spaces between the wooden pieces absorb the shock. The Daiwa is bedecked with carvings and metal ornaments just as other parts. Some mikoshi have even more imposing double-layered daiwa.

二重台輪で、棒穴のあるタイプ。
A double-layer type with beam holes.

二重ではない一般的な台輪。
A regular, single-layered daiwa.

Chapter 1: Appreciating the Design of the Mikoshi

錺金具で彩られる
台輪の装飾
Ornamental pieces that embellish daiwa

台輪紋・剃刀・台輪隅金物・棒先金物
Daiwamon, Kamisori, Daiwasumi-kanamono, Bousaki-kanamono

機能が優先される土台だが、
台輪には職人技が余すところなく盛り込まれた装飾がある。

The daiwa serves an important function and exhaustively displays the artisans' skills.

❶
紋が入った
棒先金具。
The metal cover of the beam has a crest carving.

❷
台輪の角を飾る台輪隅金具。
The corner of the daiwa is protected with golden plates.

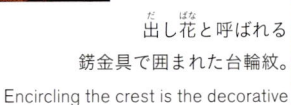

❸
出し花と呼ばれる
錺金具で囲まれた台輪紋。
Encircling the crest is the decorative part called the dashibana.

42　第1章：神輿を飾る意匠を見る

台輪にも精緻で豪華な装飾が施されている。台輪の側面には屋根紋と同じ紋章の台輪紋が刻まれている。台輪の上下にはめ込まれているギザギザの金具は剃刀と呼ばれ台輪のへりがこすれて傷まないよう保護するものだが、そのギザギザ模様さえも立派な装飾になっている。台輪の四隅には台輪の角を保護し装飾の役割もある台輪隅金物がはめ込まれている。そして担ぎ棒の先端にも保護と装飾を兼ねた棒先金物が見られる。

The daiwa is beautifully decorated just as the other parts with the yanemon crest carved on the sides. The jagged metal strip is called the kamisori (razor). While it protects the edges of the daiwa, the zigzag line is utilized as part of the design. The corners of the daiwa are also protected with decorative daiwasumi-kanamono. The edges of the carrying beams are also covered with decorative bousaki-kanamono.

台輪の上下のへりにつけられた剃刀。

The "razor" fringes the upper and lower edges of the daiwa.

棒先金物の細かい装飾。

Elaborate carvings on the end cover of the beam.

台輪隅金物と棒穴のふちに入れる覆輪(ふくりん)(右下)。

Fukurin (bottom right) will be attached to the hem of the hole for the beam.

Chapter 1: Appreciating the Design of the Mikoshi

木彫刻でより引き立つ台輪の装飾

Wooden carvings add to the aesthetic appeal of the daiwa

三味線胴・総彫り台輪
Shamisendou, Soubori-daiwa

神輿の台輪のスタイルにも流行がある。
ほんの少しの曲線が印象を変え粋な姿になる。

There are trends even in the design of daiwa.
A slight curve changes the mikoshi's impression, making it look modern.

比較的新しい時代に登場した三味線胴の台輪。
Daiwa with shamisen-dou became popular in recent years.

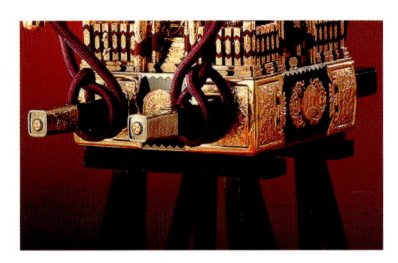

それほどふくらみが大きくない三味線胴。
Shamisen-dou with an almost straight outline.

古風ですっきりとした印象がある角台輪。
Kaku(square)-daiwa gives a classic, neat impression.

台輪の縦の線がまっすぐでふくらみがないものを角台輪と呼び、どちらかというと古風なスタイルである。それに対して比較的新しい神輿の台輪は、四隅の縦の線がゆるやかな曲線を描くようにふくらんでいる。ちょうど楽器の三味線の胴のような形をしていることから三味線胴と呼ばれ、その粋な雰囲気に人気がある。台輪の4面に台輪紋の代わりに木彫刻を入れた台輪は、総彫り台輪と呼ばれ特に手間ひまをかけた作品である。

A daiwa with a straight vertical frame is the traditional style, called kaku-daiwa. Recent mikoshi, on the other hand, have a slightly plump outline. Since it looks like the body of a Shamisen (three-stringed musical instrument), this type of frame is nicknamed Shamisen-dou and is quite popular. Some daiwa have wooden carvings on the entire surface, a work of art which requires time and effort.

天の四方を治めるという四神が彫りこまれている白木総彫り台輪。

Four mythological creatures believed to guard the four directions of the heaven are carved on the uncoated wooden daiwa.

南を治める朱雀。
Suzaku (Vermillion Bird).

東を治める青龍。 Seiryu (Blue Dragon).

北を治める玄武。
Genbu (Black Turtle entwined with a Snake).

西を治める白虎。 Byakko (White Tiger).

Chapter 1: Appreciating the Design of the Mikoshi 45

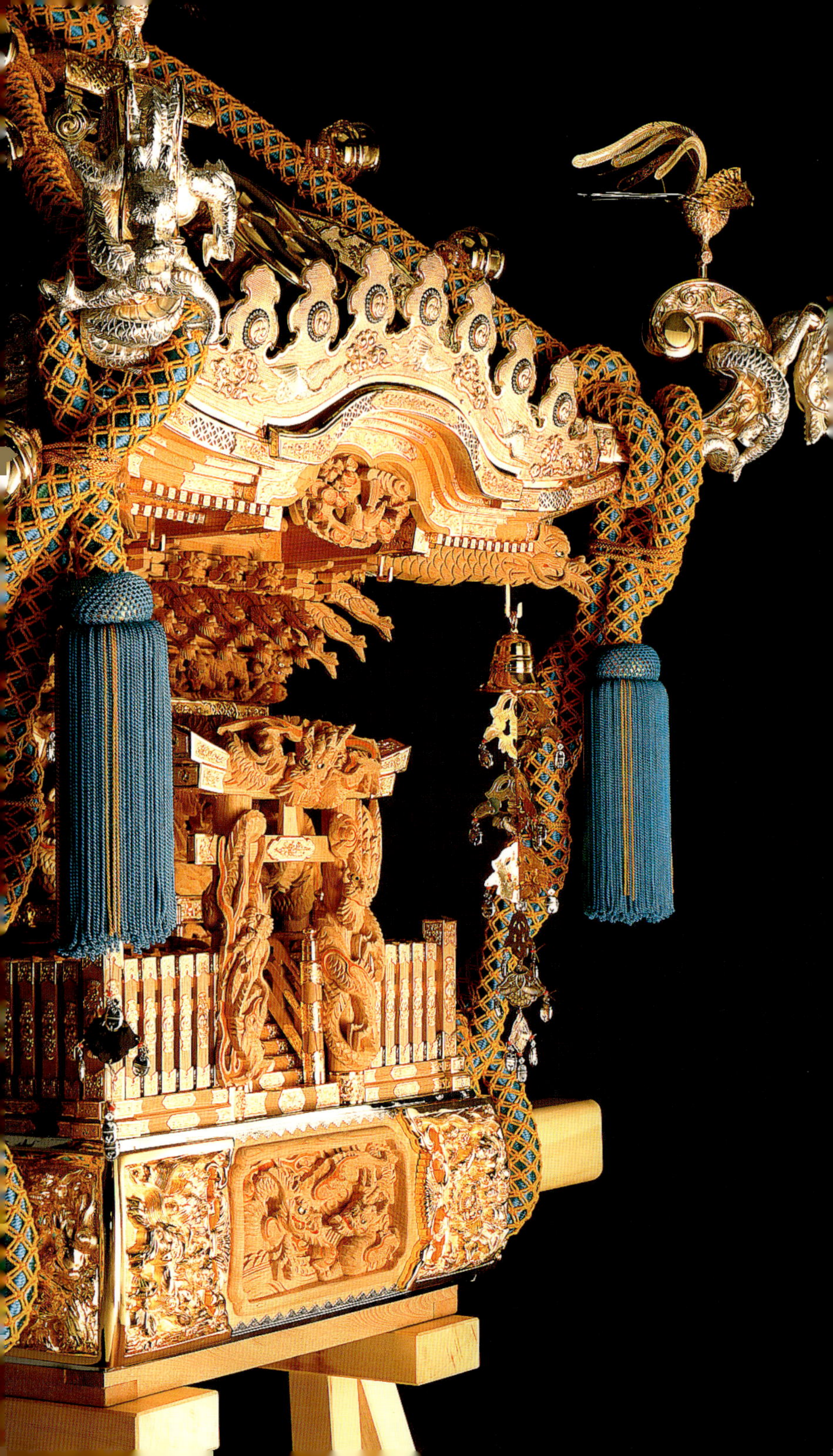

第 2 章
Chapter 2

神輿製作の職人技を知る

Learning the techniques of mikoshi construction

神輿の製作には、木地加工、鋳物、漆塗り、金箔押し、木彫刻、錺（彫金）など日本の伝統工芸の粋が集まっている。熟練の職人たちが一基の神輿を作り上げる技を見る。

The mikoshi is a compilation of Japanese traditional crafts such as woodwork, casting, lacquer work, gilding, carving, and metal work. This chapter focuses on the skills exercised by the seasoned workers in building a mikoshi.

神輿は職人技の粋の結晶

Mikoshi is the crystallization of artisanship

各地に伝わる祭りで人々の視線を一身に集める神輿は、
古来の職人技の凝縮でもある。

The mikoshi, built with ancient craftworks,
grabs the people's attention in local festivals.

木地師はカンナだけでも20種類以上を使い分ける。
Kiji-shi use more than 20 types of planes as well as other tools.

一つの神輿ができあがるまでには、どんな神輿でもおよそ1年近い年月を必要し、その工程には20種もの専門の職人が携わる。部品は細かいものまで含めれば3000にも及ぶ。木の部分の製作を担うのは木地師、鳳凰や蕨手は鋳物師、漆を塗り仕上げるのは塗師と呼ばれる漆職人、金箔は箔打ち職人、意匠を凝らした木彫刻は彫刻師、金属の板に模様を打ち出していくのは錺師によって製作される。

Building a mikoshi, regardless of its size or type, takes about a year, involving a number of experts in some 20 kinds of traditional crafts, and its components number as many as 3,000, including the various small parts. Kiji-shi build the wooden components, while the decorative pieces such as the houou and warabite are made by an imo-ji (metal caster). Nu-shi specialize in lacquer work, and goldbeaters embellish the mikoshi with gold leaf stamping. The mikoshi also let us admire the work of wood sculptors and kazari-shi, who make the reliefs on the metal ornaments.

おもな製作工程　Main steps in building a mikoshi

カンナなどによる木地の加工、漆塗り、木彫刻、錺など日本の伝統技術が結集して、一基の神輿が作られる。

In building a mikoshi, various kinds of artisanship, including wood processing with planes, lacquer coating, carving, and metal chasing are called for.

木地加工　Processing of wooden parts

神輿のあらゆる木の部分の製作と加工と組み立てを担う。

Make and assemble all the wooden components of the mikoshi

木彫刻　Carving

台輪や鳥居など木でできている部分に精巧な彫刻を施す。

Add elaborate carving to wooden components, such as the daiwa and torii

錺　Kazari

各部分にある装飾用、保護・補強用の金属の板に細かい模様を打ち出す。

Create detailed reliefs on metal parts for decoration, protection and reinforcement.

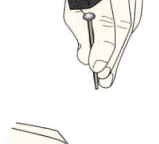

鋳物　Casting

鳳凰や蕨手は型に金属を流し込む鋳物で製作する。

Cast metal to create parts, such as the houou and warabite.

漆塗り　Lacquer coating

屋根などに伝統工芸の漆を塗り、磨き、仕上げる。

Coat the roof and other parts with lacquer and polish.

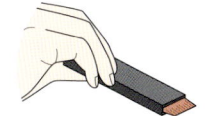

木地部製作のための木工工具

Wood processing tools

神輿の主要部分は木で作られる。
伝統工具の一つひとつに役割があり、職人の魂が伝わる。

A large portion of the mikoshi is made of wood.
Each tool serves a different purpose and conveys the craftsman's soul.

荒取りや接合部を切るのに使用するノコギリ類。一番下は指矩(さしがね)。

Saws are used to cut out a block and sever joints. On the bottom is sashigane (carpenter's square).

カンナは平面を削るだけでなく曲面やごく細かい部分にも使う。

Planes are used not only for smoothing a flat or curved surface, but also for making delicate carvings.

神輿づくりのための工具類は、基本的に日本の伝統建築に使用される道具と同様である。ノコギリは、元の材木から切り出す荒取り用のものや、曲線を切るためのものなどがある。カンナは、カンナ身と呼ばれる刃と木製のカンナ台からなり、平面、材料の際、溝、曲面など削る場所によって多くの種類がある。ノミは、おもに穴を掘るため工具で、刃の反対側をゲンノウ（鉄製の大きな鎚）で叩いて使う。穴の形状に合わせて刃の種類は多様である。

Tools for building the mikoshi are basically the same as those used in traditional Japanese architecture, and each comes in a large variety. Take the saw, for example, some are used for cutting out a block from a log, while others are made to cut a piece along a curve. Another major tool is the plane, which is composed of a blade, a wooden base, as well as other parts. Different types are used for smoothing a flat surface, a curved surface, scraping an edge, and making a groove. The chisel is mainly used for carving a hole. The blade is stuck vertically on the wood and the other end is hammered. There is even a large variety of chisels, which are used to make holes of different shapes and sizes.

木材に罫線を引くための道具、罫引。

Kebiki are used to draw ruled lines on wood.

ノミは常に研がれる。工具を研ぐのも職人の重要な仕事。

Chisels are kept sharpened at all times. Whetting the tools is an important part of work for craftsmen.

神輿に適した木材の選定

Choosing the appropriate wood

細工の施しやすさと激しい動きに耐える堅牢さが、
神輿製作の木材選びに求められる。

Ease of processing and durability against violent jolts are the key points in choosing the right wood for mikoshi.

板状に切断された木は最低でもふた夏は乾燥させる。

Wood plates must be dried for at least two summers.

仕上げや使う部分で木材の種類を選ぶ。

An appropriate wood is chosen depending on how and in which part it will be used.

神輿の主要部分は木で作られるが、仕上げ方によって種類は変わる。塗装を施さない白木神輿は、美しい木目、堅さ、強さが特徴の国産のケヤキ材が最適とされる。漆塗り神輿は、ケヤキに比べてしなやかさが特徴のヒノキやホウが使われることが多い。伐り出した木材はそのまま加工すると縮んだり反ったりするので、少しずつ乾燥させる。神輿作りに使用する木材は、約3年間は倉庫の中で乾燥させながら大切に保管される。

Among several types of wood, the most appropriate one is chosen depending on the type of mikoshi. Domestic zelkova, which is characterized by beautiful grain, hardness and strength, is considered the best choice for a shiraki mikoshi, which features a white, uncoated surface of wood. For lacquered mikoshi, on the other hand, more flexible varieties like hinoki cypress and hou (Japanese big-leaf magnolia) are preferred. The cut out wood must be dried slowly before use in order to prevent shrinkage and bending. The wood used for mikoshi is normally kept in storage with great care for about three years.

木目の形状や詰まり具合は木を選ぶための大事な判断材料になる。
The grain's shape and fineness are important criteria for choosing wood.

❖ 神輿に使われる木材　Popular kinds of wood for mikoshi

ケヤキ　Zelkova
堅く強い木材で木目の美しさが特徴。太鼓の胴や生活用具などに使用される。
Hard and strong. With a beautiful grain, often used to make Japanese drums and various kinds of livingware.

ホウ　Hou (Japanese big-leaf magnolia)
木目がまっすぐなのが特徴。比較的や軟らかいので細かい彫刻など精密な加工がしやすい。
Has a characteristic straight grain. Relatively soft and well suited for detailed carving.

ヒノキ　Hinoki (Japanese cypress)
社寺建築をはじめとして、日本建築には欠かせない高級木材。加工しやすく、耐水性に優れている。独特の芳香も魅力。
A high-end, indispensable material for temples, shrines and other Japanese structures. Known for its fine aroma, it is easy to process and excels in water resistance.

カシ　Oak
堅く耐久性に優れている。カンナ台や太鼓のばちとしても使われる。神輿では強度が必要な部分に使う。
Hard and excels in durability. Often used in the base of a planing tool and in plectrums for drums. Used for the parts of the mikoshi where strength is required.

社寺建築も神輿製作も図面は原寸で描かれる

Full-sized drawings are used in building a temple, shrine or mikoshi

日本の社寺建築から意匠や技法の流れを汲む神輿製作では、図面もそれにならっている。

The mikoshi is modeled after the architecture of Japanese temples and shrines in the design and techniques, as well as in the drawings.

日本古来の社寺建築の図面は、縮小された設計図だけではなく、手書きで原寸大に描く「原寸図」も作成された。現在でも、屋根の勾配などを調整するため、ベニヤ板などに原寸図を描く作業は行われている。実際の大きさに描くので、広い体育館のような場所が必要だというほどである。宮大工は原寸図が書けなければ一人前とはみなしてもらえないのだという。社寺建築の流れを汲む神輿でも、図面は原寸大で描かれる。神輿の場合は左右対称という特徴もあり、ちょうど半面ずつが一枚の紙に描かれる。木地師はそれをもとに、神輿の主要部分を作成するのである。

In building a traditional Japanese structure like a temple or a shrine, it was and is customary to use not only a blueprint in a reduced scale, but also a full-sized drawing. Even today, builders often draw a life-sized plan on plywood to determine the angle of the roof, a procedure which needs a large space like a gymnasium. It is said miyadaiku (carpenters specializing in temples and shrines) are not considered full-fledged until they are able to draw a life-sized design. Mikoshi builders also use a full-sized drawing. Since the mikoshi is built in a symmetric form, a half of the structure is drawn on a piece of paper, based on which kiji-shi will create the major wooden parts of the mikoshi.

1枚の中にいくつもの要素を入れるが、どの部分も左右対称であるため半分ずつが描かれる。

Various elements are included in the drawing. Since all the parts are symmetric, only half of the mikoshi is drawn.

重量と衝撃に耐える
堅固な台輪(だいわ)

Solid daiwa endure weight and shock

重量に耐え、大勢の担ぎ手の動きを受け止めるため、
しなやかさと強さが求められる。

Flexibility and strength are required to support the mikoshi's weight even when it is bouncing on the carriers' shoulders.

神輿の重量は150kgから、大きな物では鋳物、錺金具、担ぎ棒も含めると1t以上もの重さになるものもある。この重量を支え、しかも担ぎ棒が通されることで衝撃はじかに伝わるため台輪はとても堅固に作られている。台輪もほかの木地部分と同様に製作の際には日本の伝統的な建築技術である組み木で接合される。鉄くぎを使わず「ほぞ」で接合されるため接合部に微妙なすき間である「遊び」が生まれ、衝撃を吸収することで、重量にも衝撃にも耐えるのである。

The weight of mikoshi ranges from 150 kilograms to over 1 ton with all the cast parts, ornaments and carrying beams included. To support the enormous weight and absorb the shocks directly conveyed from the beams, daiwa must be robustly constructed. As in other wooden parts, the daiwa is built with the Japanese traditional architectural technique, known as kumiki (wood assembling). By joining a tenon and a mortise together without using iron nails, narrow spaces remain between the wood, which absorb impacts and bear the mikoshi's weight and vibration.

台輪の組み立て前の部材。真ん中の2つの板には棒穴があり、両側の2つの板の盛り上がっている部分に彫刻が施される。

Parts of a daiwa before assembling. The two plates in the middle have holes through which beams will be inserted. Carvings will be applied on the elevated parts of the two plates on both ends.

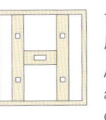

台輪の骨組みを上から見た図。屋根の骨組みと似ている。

A daiwa frame viewed from directly above. It looks similar to the frame of a roof.

周囲を囲む厚い板にある四角い穴は、担ぎ棒を通す穴。

The square holes on the outer frame are for inserting the carrying beams.

上部に板をはめ込んで組み立てた台輪。

Daiwa completed with the top plate.

神輿の壮麗な屋根を支える骨組み

Framework to support the mikoshi's enormous roof

祭りで人々に担がれているときに一番目立つ屋根。
装飾が施される前の骨組みは堅牢である。

The roof is the most eye-catching part when the mikoshi is being carried during the matsuri (festival).
Hidden beneath the colorful ornaments is a robust frame.

唐破風屋根を組み立てるのに必要な部材の一部。

Some of the parts that will compose a karahafu roof.

できあがると見えなくなってしまう屋根の骨組みだが、内部は緻密且つ堅牢に構成されている。真ん中には、台輪から屋根までを貫き通して支える芯柱(しんばしら)と、四隅の四本柱(しほんばしら)を通す厚板があり、それを囲むようにいくつもの部材が組み合わされる。屋根の骨組みは、正確に均衡のとれた形状で、些細な凹凸が生じることは許されない。そのため木地師は木組みの際に何度も微調整を繰り返し、ノミとカンナを使い分け時間をかけて仕上げるのである。

The roof's framework, though it becomes invisible after the mikoshi is completed, is meticulously designed and strongly built. Right in the middle is a thick plate that will support the core pillar and four corner pillars, and other components are attached to surround this plate. The frame of the roof is a symmetrical form and allows no room for even the tiniest distortion. Kiji-shi, therefore, painstakingly keep making one fine adjustment after another, with chisels and planes, until a perfect frame is created.

芯柱を中心に
放射状に広がる屋根の骨格。

The framework spreads radially from the core pillar.

中心に芯柱を通す穴が空いた板、その周囲に堂の四本柱を通す穴が空いた板が組み合わされる。

A plate with a hole for the core pillar and two other plates with holes for the corner pillars are fixed together.

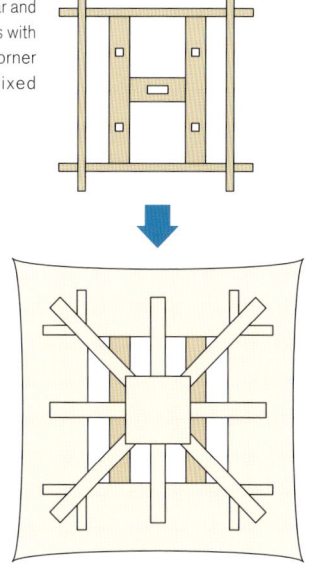

屋根を真上から見た状態。軒下の板が張られ、芯柱から放射状に骨組みが広がる。

A roof viewed from directly above. The frame spreads on the eave plates in a radial fashion from the core pillar.

Chapter 2: Appreciating the Design of the Mikoshi

屋根の形状を決定づける野地板(のじいた)張り

Nojiita-bari determines the shape of the roof

下から上へ屋根の曲面に沿って野地板を張る。
その仕上がりのよさが漆塗り工程にも影響する。

Nojiita plates are laid from the bottom up along the curved surface of the roof.
Its outcome influences the lacquering process which follows.

野地板は何度も削られて滑らかな表面に仕上げる。
Nojiita are scraped over and over until the surface becomes smooth.

屋根の骨組みが完成したら、骨組み全体を覆うように野地板を張っていく。野地板は、あとから漆塗りで仕上げる際の部材であるため、張る際にも仕上げにも狂いや凹凸のない緻密さが要求される。野地板の一枚一枚は、端の曲面をノミで削って調整しつつ、下から上へと張り合わせていく。張り終えたら、何度も微調整を繰り返しながらカンナをかけ、まるで最初からゆるやかな曲面の一枚の板ででもあったかのように、滑らかに仕上げるのである。

Once the roof frame is finished, it is covered by plates called nojiita. Since the plates will be coated with lacquer later, meticulous attention is paid to attach them without deviation, bumps or dents. Each plate is placed from bottom to top, and fine adjustments are made with a chisel, so that they perfectly fit the curve. Once they are fixed to the frame, the surface is smoothed with a plane over and over until they become like a single plate, curving gently along the frame.

野地板の端の傾斜はノミで削られて形が整えられる。

The edges of the nojiita are carefully chiseled.

屋根の骨組みの外側に野地板を一枚ずつ張っていく。一枚ごとに形状も大きさも異なる。

Nojiita are placed one by one on the frame of the roof. Each plate is made in a different shape and size.

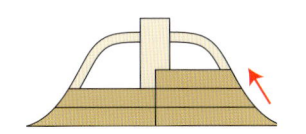

野地板は下から順番に張る。屋根の微妙な曲線に合わせるのは熟練が必要。

Nojiita are attached from bottom to top. Fixing the plates on the roof's subtle curves requires particular skill.

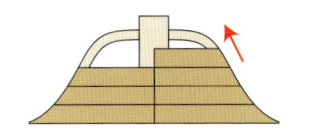

４つの面に野地板を張り終えたらていねいにカンナを掛けて仕上げる。

Once the plates are placed on all four sides, the surface is thoroughly smoothed with a plane.

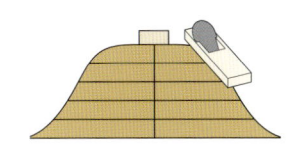

装飾と機能性を兼ね備える桝組み

Masugumi serves decorative and functional purposes

屋根を支える桝組みは、美しい装飾であるばかりでなく、
衝撃から屋根を守る機能をもつ。

The beautifully assembled Masugumi protects the roof from impacts.

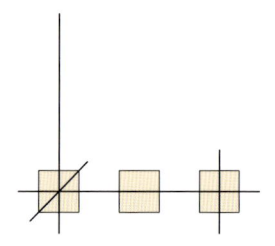

縦横斜めに走っている直線が肘木。右は十文字の肘木を支える巻桝。真ん中は1本の肘木だけを支える延桝。左は十文字と斜めの肘木の角の交差を支える角桝。

Hijiki are laid in vertical, horizontal and diagonal directions. On the right is makimasu, which supports crossing hijiki, while nobemasu in the center holds only one hijiki. On the left is kadomasu, which is used at the intersection of three crossing hijiki.

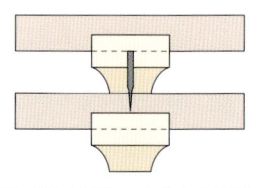

2段に組んだ桝組みを横から透視したところ。一番上の肘木はすぐ下の桝に接着されずに載っている。その桝は下の肘木と竹くぎで固定されている。

Perspective view of two tiers of masugumi. The hijiki on the top are laid on the masu, but not glued. The masu, however, is fixed onto the hijiki below with bamboo nails.

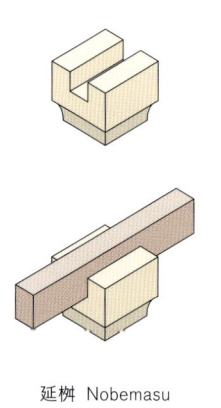

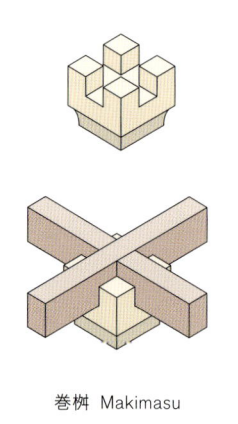

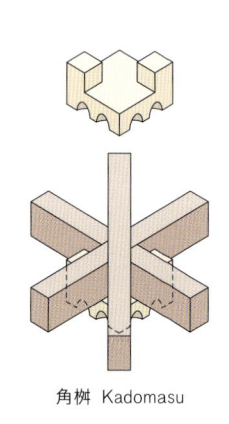

延桝 Nobemasu

巻桝 Makimasu

角桝 Kadomasu

神輿の屋根は桝組み（組み物）で支えられている。堂に比べて大きく張り出した屋根を支え、上下左右に大きく揺らされる衝撃を吸収することができる。たくさんの桝と肘木で構成されている桝組みの、桝に載る肘木は桝とは接着されていない。このためここに「遊び」が生まれて振動に耐えることができる。肘木の上に来る桝とは竹くぎで固定されている。真横から見ると、桝の下に肘木が固定された組み合わせで１段の桝組みとなる。これが何段か固定されずに重なり、下の段にいくにしたがって少しずつ小さくなる。

The mikoshi's roof rests on the masugumi, which supports the weight of the roof extending above the dou, and absorbs the impacts when the mikoshi is tossed up and down, left and right. The masugumi is composed of dozens of masu (blocks) and hijiki (sticks). The hijiki are not glued to the masu below to allow space to absorb vibration. The masu, however, are fixed to the lower hijiki with bamboo nails. Looking from the side, each tier is composed of masu and hijiki layers, which is placed on top of another, smaller tier.

先端部分に龍が彫ってある凝った作りの桝組み。

Masugimi with elaborate dragon carvings.

長短いくつもの肘木や何種類もの桝など膨大な数の部材が必要。

An enormous number of parts including hijiki in various lengths and many kinds of masu are required.

小さな桝の一つひとつにカンナを掛ける。

Each of the small masu is planed carefully.

Chapter 2: Appreciating the Design of the Mikoshi

木地師の確かな仕事が骨格を作る

Kiji-shi's mastery completes the framework

神輿作りで木地師の仕事は、
神輿の骨格部分から装飾的な部材まで多岐にわたる。
Kiji-shi's tasks range from the mikoshi's framework to decorative parts.

4つに分けて製作された囲垣の部材。
The four sections will be assembled to make an igaki.

屋根、堂、台輪の主要な3つの部分とこれらを貫く芯柱、そして桝組みは、神輿の骨組みとなる構造上の最重要部分であり、いずれも熟練の木地師によって製作される。一方、装飾として、あるいは祈りの気持ちが込められた部分も神輿にはたくさん存在している。神社の本殿や回廊を囲む勾欄、階、鳥居や囲垣など、精巧な模型のようなこれらもすべても職人が一つひとつ作った木地部分だ。

The mikoshi's three main sections, namely the roof, the dou, and the daiwa, as well as the core pillar and the masugumi are the most important parts of the structure, and all of these are created by experienced kiji-shi. There are also many smaller parts, some of which serve a decorative purpose, while others represent prayers offered to the kami. The components like kouran, kizahashi, torii, igaki are accurate miniatures of the objects around the shrine's main hall or corridor, and these are also made one by one by time-served wood workers.

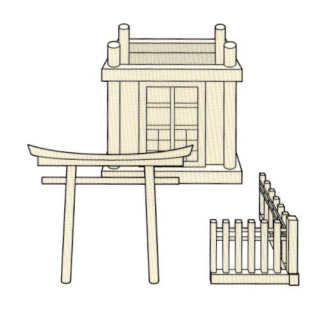

堂、囲垣、鳥居などたくさんの木地加工された部材が使われている。

The dou, the igaki, and the torii are among many wooden components.

階に取りつける手すりも本物そっくりの模型のようだ。

The hand rails of the kizahashi look exactly like those in the shrine.

各部材を台輪の上に仮組みするとそれぞれの部材の役割が分かってくる。

By placing the parts tentatively on the daiwa, it is easy to see each component's role in the miniature shrine.

Chapter 2: Appreciating the Design of the Mikoshi

鋳物によって作られる
鳳凰と蕨手

Houou and warabite made by metal casting

鋳物は人類が古くから用いてきた技術。
神輿では鳳凰や蕨手などに古来の技法が用いられる。

Humans have been using metal casting techniques since ancient times; it is also essential in creating the houou and warabite.

鋳型の中で冷えて固まった蕨手。
Warabite cooled down in a mold.

鋳物は細かい造形も表現することができる。
Expressing elaborate design with metal casting.

鳳凰や蕨手などは鋳物師の手によって作られる鋳物である。鋳物は古代からある金属成型技術で、熱して溶かした金属を型穴に流し入れて固める。神輿の鋳物は、まず木彫刻の職人が木型(きがた)を作る。枠の中にこの木型を入れて周囲を砂で固めてひっくり返して木型を取り除くと鋳型(いがた)ができる。鋳型は片面ずつをそれぞれ作り、それを合わせて、中の空間に溶かした金属を流し込む。神輿の蕨手には真鍮(しんちゅう)が用いられる。冷えて固まった鋳物は磨いて仕上げる。

The metal parts such as the houou and the warabite are made by an imo-ji (metal caster). Metal casting is an old technique, in which metal is melted by heat, poured into a mold and solidified by cooling. The first step in the creation of the mikoshi's metal parts involves a wood carver who creates a pattern. The wood pattern is then placed in a frame, and the space filled with sand. Once the sand becomes solid, the frame is turned upside down and the pattern is removed to complete a mold, which represents a half of the form to be created. Two molds representing each half are joined and metal is poured into the empty space. After the metal is cooled and becomes solid, it is taken out from the frame and finished by polishing. Normally, brass is used as the material for the warabite.

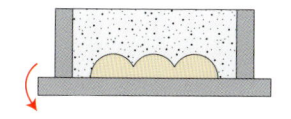

完成する鋳物と同じ彫刻が施された木型を枠に入れて砂で固め、ひっくり返して取り除くと鋳型ができる。

An exact pattern is created with wood and placed in a box. The space is filled with sand and pressured to solidify. Then, the box is turned upside down to remove the pattern.

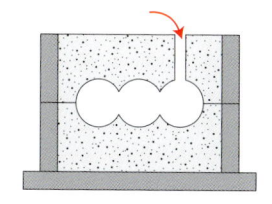

鋳型は片面ずつ作り、それを合わせると中に木型と同じ空間ができる。ここに溶かした金属を流し込む。

Two molds are used to create one piece. Metal is poured into the space in the molds.

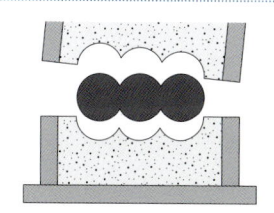

流し込まれた金属が固まったら中から取り出す。表面を磨くなどして仕上げれば鋳物の部材が完成する。

Once the metal becomes solid, it is taken out and the surface is polished.

漆だけがもつ特性を
生かす工具類

Tools maximize a lacquer's characteristics

漆は古くから生活に密着した素材であり、
海外でも珍重される高級な工芸作品の材料である。

Lacquer has been a part of the Japanese people's lives since early times, and also treasured overseas as a material of high-end crafts.

漆を練ったり、下地作業・下塗り・中塗りなどに使用される木や竹のへら。

Wooden and bamboo hera are used to knead lacquer and to apply the base coating, the under layer and the middle layer.

漆は漆の木の樹液から作られ、接着・保護剤としての機能と、何よりもその美しい色と艶が珍重される。神輿の漆塗りは、下地作業・下塗り・中塗り・上塗り・仕上げ塗りに大きく分けられ、それぞれに異なったいくつもの工具が使われる。ヘラは顔料と漆を練り合わせたり下地塗りをしたりするのに使う。塗ハケの毛は人毛が使われ、毛がすり減ったら木の部分を切り新しい毛を出して使う。このためハケの中にはずっと奥まで毛が入っている。

Made of urushi resin, lacquer has been valued for its functionality as an adhesive and protection material. But its fascinating color and sleek texture are probably the reasons it is so greatly prized. Lacquer coating of mikoshi roughly consists of five steps and various tools are used in each step. For example, hera, wooden sticks with a flat end, are used to mix a colorant and lacquer and to apply a base coating. The lacquer brushes are made of human hair. As the tip wears down, the wooden part is trimmed to let the brush come out. For this, the hair is inserted all the way down the handle.

新品の状態のハケ（一番左）と、ハケそのものに漆を塗ったもの（真ん中の２つ）。細い筆も細かい作業では使う。

A brand new brush (right) and brushes with their handles lacquered (two in the middle). The thin brushes are used on detailed parts.

一番左はヘラを削る塗師包丁、丸ノミは下地作業の刻苧彫りに使う。刻苧とはケヤキの粉末と漆を混ぜ合わせた一種の接着剤である。右の２本の切り出しはハケを削るのに使う。

On the left is a special knife to sharpen hera. The round chisel is used in the base-coating phase to apply an adhesive called kokuso, which is made of a mixture of powdered zelkova wood and lacquer. The two knifes on the right are used to shorten the handle of the brushes.

Chapter 2: Appreciating the Design of the Mikoshi

漆塗りの基礎となる下地作業
Foundation coating for lacquer work

屋根を漆塗りで仕上げるには強度と仕上げを左右する下地作業が重要である。
The base coat determines the roof's strength and appearance.

野地板の合わせ目に溝を掘り、刻苧と細く切った布を一緒に埋めていく。
Grooves are carved along the joints of nojiita and filled with strips of hemp and kokuso.

神輿の屋根は漆塗りで仕上げることが多く、面積も広いことからその工程には多くの時間を割く。最初の工程は下地作業で、野地板の継ぎ目の割れを防ぐ目的がある。まず板の合わせ目に丸ノミで一直線に溝を彫る。この溝に、刻苧と一緒に細く切った麻布を塗り込めるように埋めて平面にする。そして屋根全体に麻布をかぶせて下地漆を塗る。

Many mikoshi roofs are lacquer-coated, and because of the large surface area, applying lacquer on the roof is a time-consuming process. The first step is the base coating, which makes the surface of the nojiita seamless. Straight grooves are carved with a gouge along the joints of the nojiita plates, and filled with thin strips of hemp and kokuso. Then, the entire roof is covered with hemp cloth, on which the base coating will be applied.

未精製の漆はクリーム色をしている。
Unrefined lacquer is cream-colored.

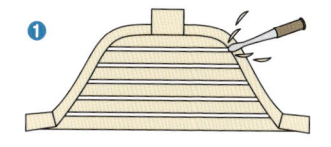

❶ 野地板の合わせ目の上を、小型の丸ノミで溝を掘るところから塗師の仕事となる。
Lacquerers work begins with carving grooves with a small gouge along the joint lines.

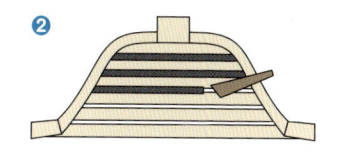

❷ 一本ずつの溝に、刻苧と一緒に細く切った麻布をヘラで埋め込んでいく。
Using hera, each groove is filled with strips of hemp and kokuso.

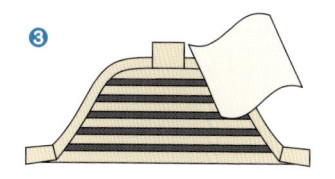

❸ 溝を刻苧ですっかり埋めたら、屋根全体に大きな麻布をかぶせて下地漆を全面に塗る。
Once the grooves are completely filled, the roof is covered with large sections of hemp cloth on which the base lacquer is applied.

下塗り・中塗りを
ていねいに

No pains spared in applying the base and middle coatings

塗る・乾かす・磨く。その繰り返しが漆独特の風合いと光沢を生み出す。
Repetition of coating, drying and polishing
creates the lacquer's characteristic texture and gloss.

未精製の漆の液を和紙にくるんで絞り、和紙の微細な穴に漆だけを透過させ、
不純物を取り除いて精製する。

Unrefined lacquer is wrapped in washi paper and squeezed.
The paper, with its fine texture, filters the lacquer and removes impurities.

漆塗りの下地作業に続いて下塗りが行なわれる。その目的は、布と木地の段差や境目を消し、全体を滑らかにすることである。下塗り用の漆を塗って、乾燥させ、磨いて表面を平滑にする作業が数回にわたって繰り返される。下塗りにはヘラが使われ、研磨には砥石や炭が使われる。次は中塗りである。中塗り以降は精製された漆が使われる。また、ここからはヘラではなくハケを使う。中塗りでも塗り・乾燥・研磨が繰り返される。

After the base is made, a first coating is added to smooth the surface, eliminating seams and bumps on the cloth and on the wood. Then, the cloth is daubed with unrefined lacquer, which will be dried and polished to make the surface even. This procedure is repeated several times. Hera is used for coating, while rubbing stones and coal are employed for polishing. This process is followed by a middle coating. In the middle and upper coatings, refined lacquer is applied with brushes, instead of hera. As in the first step, coating, drying and polishing are repeated.

下塗りをした鳥居。
Torii after the base coating is applied.

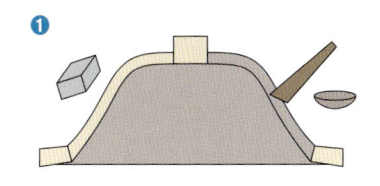

❶
ヘラを使って下塗りの漆を全体に塗る。塗って、乾かしたら、砥石を使って表面の凹凸がなくなるまでていねいに磨く。

Using hera, the whole roof is coated with a base lacquer. Once it dries, the surface is carefully smoothed with a rubbing stone.

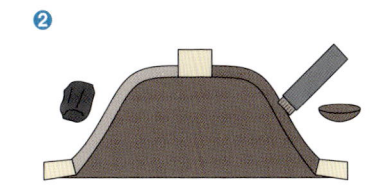

❷
下塗りを繰り返した後、中塗りをする。塗るのはハケを使う。乾燥させたら炭で磨き、さらに塗り・乾燥・研磨を繰り返す。

After several rounds of base coating, the middle coat is applied with a brush. Once the lacquer is dried, it will be polished with coal, and the same procedure will be repeated.

漆塗りの最終工程
上塗り・仕上げ塗り

Final coating completes the lacquering process

漆塗りは日本を代表する工芸の一つ。
長い時間と手間をかけてついに漆塗りが完成する。

Lacquer work is one of the Japanese peoples' most prominent traditional crafts. Workers devote substantial time and effort to lacquer coating.

塗っては乾かす工程を経て深い光沢が生み出される。

The repetition of coating and drying creates a deep luster.

漆を乾燥させる漆室(塗師室ともいう)は、湿度と温度が管理されている。

Lacquer is dried in a room called urushimuro (lacquer room) or nurimuro (coating room), where the humidity and temperature are controlled.

中塗りに続く上塗り・仕上げ塗りの作業も、ホコリがつかないよう、より清浄な部屋の中で行なわれる。それぞれに専用のハケが使われ、漆も念入りに精製される。漆の乾燥には湿度が必要で、乾燥させるために湿度が必要な塗料はほかに例がないといわれる。上塗りでも、塗り・乾燥・研磨が繰り返され、仕上げ塗りに移る。仕上げ塗りには徹底的な研磨で艶を出す「呂色仕上げ」など高度な技法がある。漆塗りの美しさは、複雑で長い工程を経て完成する。

Once the middle coating is finished, an upper and final coating are added in a clean room to prevent dust from falling on the coated surface. Different types of brushes are used for the upper coating and final coating, and the lacquer is carefully refined in advance. In order to dry the lacquer, the air must be humidified to a certain extent. Lacquer is said to be the only coating material that requires humidity to dry. The coating-drying-polishing procedure is repeated again before the final coating step, in which the lacquer will be thoroughly polished to achieve the utmost luster. Using sophisticated methods such as roiro finishing, which brings about extreme sleekness, the long, painstaking lacquer work is completed.

高級品になると漆の上に金粉をまいて仕上げることもある。

Some high-end products are finished with gold powder.

❶ 漆を塗ったら漆室に入れて"湿気で乾燥"させる。漆室は湿度は75〜80％、温度は20〜30℃に保たれている。

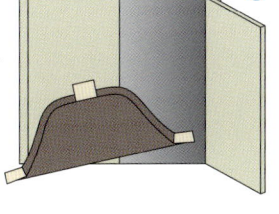

The lacquer-coated roof is moved into the urushimuro to "dry in humidity." The humidity in the room is maintained at 75 - 80%, and the temperature at 20 - 30 degrees Celsius.

❷ 漆を塗り、乾燥させて、研磨する。研磨では、ごく微細な研磨剤をつけて布で丁寧に磨く。

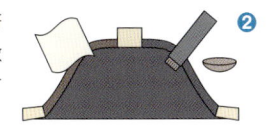

Coating, drying and polishing are repeated. Using a cloth and an abrasive with fine grain, the lacquer is polished with extreme care.

❸ 丹念に磨かれた漆は、すばらしく深みのある艶と色に仕上がる。

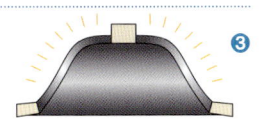

By polishing elaborately, a rich luster and thick tone are achieved.

神輿を絢爛豪華に彩る金箔
けんらんごうか

Gold leaf adds to the mikoshi's splendor

神輿の装飾技法の中でも、とりわけ豪華なのが
箔打ち職人による金箔押しの仕上げである。

Particularly luxurious among the mikoshi's decorations
is the gold leaf stamping.

三社型神輿の軒下と桝組み部分に金箔が施されている。

The eaves and masugumi of the Sanja-style mikoshi with gold leaf.

白木神輿の金箔仕上げは一味違った豪華さが魅力。

On a while-wood mikoshi, gold leaf stamping creates a distinct beauty.

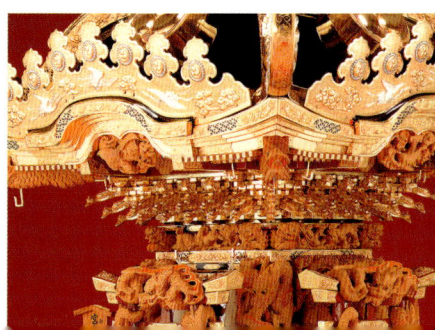

金箔は1万分の1〜2mmの薄さまで伸ばすことができる。わずか2gの金が畳1枚分ほどの大きさまで延ばされる計算だ。これは金の性質と、日本の箔打ち職人のすぐれた伝統技術による。神輿を見たときに、金色に光っているところの多くは錺金具による装飾で、金箔押しを施すのは、桝組みや屋根の軒の裏側部分である。桝組みや軒(のき)を金箔によって仕上げる場合は、箔下漆(はくしたうるし)を塗ってから金箔押しや金粉を施す。

Gold can be beaten into an extreme thinness of about 1/10,000th or 2/10,000ths of a millimeter. A mere 2 grams of gold can be enlarged to the size of a tatami mat. This is possible because of the characteristics of gold combined with Japanese goldbeaters' excellent skills. In the mikoshi, in addition to many glittering ornaments, gold leaf stamping is often used to embellish the masugumi and the underside of the eaves. Before applying gold leaf or gold powder on a component, its surface is coated with lacquer.

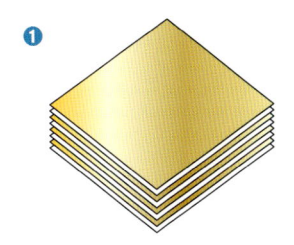

❶ 製造された金箔は紙に交互にはさまって、100枚ほどが重なって販売されている。さまざまな品質や厚さのものがある。

Gold leaf is normally sold in a set of about 100 pieces and comes in various qualities and thicknesses. The pieces are held between sheets of paper.

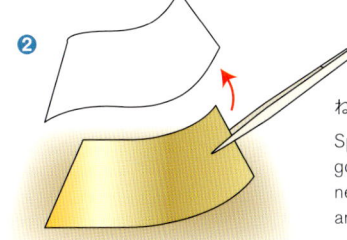

❷ 金箔を紙と分離して張る場所へ移し替えるには、金箔工芸専用の竹製の箔箸(はくばし)を使い、ていねいに一枚ずつ扱う。

Special bamboo chopsticks are used to peel off a gold leaf from the paper and move it to the area it needs to be stamped. With great caution the pieces are moved one at a time.

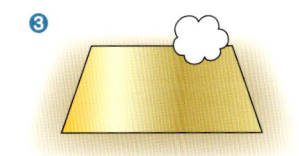

❸ 張りつけた金箔は、わたなどを使って密着させる。桝組みなど複雑な形状の部分に張るには高度な技術が必要だ。

The leaf is fixed to the surface by rubbing with cotton or other materials. A high skill is called for in decorating a complicated part such as the masugumi.

技の数だけ存在する木彫刻工具

As many carving tools as the number of techniques

木彫刻を工芸芸術の域に高めるのは、
職人の腕と、技法ごとに使い分けられる無数の工具による。

Craftsmen's skills and innumerable tools are exercised
to heighten wood carving to the level of fine art.

平ノミの数々。写真左から右へ、刃の幅の広いものから狭いものへ並んでいる。
平ノミもこれですべてではない。

Chisels with a flat blade. The left-most one has the widest blade, which gets smaller moving toward the right. These are just a small sample of flat chisels.

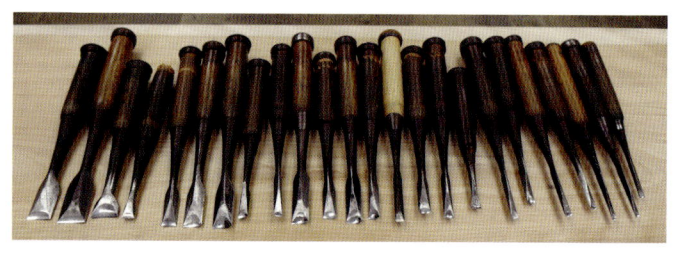

すべて外丸ノミ。写真左から右へ、刃の幅が広く、
アールの小さいものから大きいものへ並んでいる。ほかに内丸ノミもある。

Chisels with a round blade for whittling a convex line. The leftmost one has the widest blade with a small curve, and the ones on the right have narrower blades with sharper curves. There are also just as many chisels with round blades to whittle grooves.

木彫刻に使用するのは、おもにノミと仕上げノミである。一般に、ノミは刃を木部にあて、冠のついた柄をゲンノウや木ヅチで打って使う「たたきノミ」が主である。一方、仕上げノミは手に握って使うもので彫刻刀とも呼ばれる。ノミは刃の形のままの彫り跡ができるので、彫る幅・深さ・形に深さによって平ノミ・内丸ノミ・外丸ノミ・三角ノミなどノミの種類を変えながら作業をする。仕上げノミにもとても多くの種類があり使い分けられる。

Wood carvers mainly use chisels, which are roughly classified into two types. The normal chisel is used by applying the blade to the wood and hammering the other end. The so-called finishing chisel, on the other hand, is held in the hand to engrave the wood directly. Since chisels make distinct cuts according to the shape of the blade, workers use a myriad of chisels. Some have a flat blade, while others have a three-cornered blade. There are also chisels with a round blade to whittle grooves and also elevated lines. The best-suited one is chosen according to the width, depth and shape of the cut they want to make. There is also a great variety of finishing chisels.

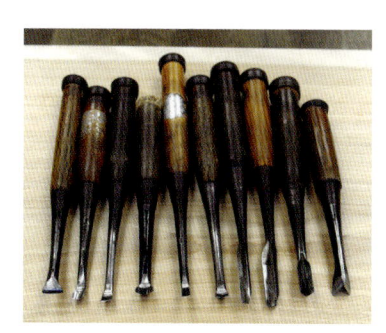

丸刃ノミと三角ノミ。
Chisels with a round blade and a three-cornered blade.

多種類の仕上げノミ。小刀、切り出しノミ、平ノミ、外丸ノミ、曲がりノミ、三角ノミなどがある。
Among the finishing chisels are small knives, chisels with a flat blade, a round blade for whittling a projection, a curved blade, and a three-cornered blade.

木彫刻で
神輿が生きた造形に

Wood carving gives life to the mikoshi

最初は一本の木である。
木彫師がそこに何かを探り当ててノミを打ち込み魂を生み出す。

Sculptor's inspiration and chisels create a soul out of a piece of wood.

木彫刻師の仕事風景。
ずらりと並んでいる道具の位置はその職人だけに分かる特有のもの。

A wood carver in his workshop with a host of tools.
A master craftsman knows exactly where each tool is.

木彫刻の工程を専門に行う職人は木彫刻師または木彫師と呼ばれる。神輿では台輪や堂の部分を中心として木地に多くの彫刻を施す。手の込んだものになると木地が彫刻で埋め尽くされた印象となり総彫りとも呼ばれるほどである。木彫の主材料となる木材は主にケヤキが使われる。部位によって製作方法は異なるが、たとえば龍が巻きついた鳥居は、鳥居と龍を別々に作って後からはめ込むのではなく、龍と鳥居を一本の木から同時に彫り出す。

The carvings in the wooden parts in mikoshi, mainly around the daiwa and dou, are the work of wood carvers. In some cases, the entire surface of the major wooden parts are covered by elaborate carvings, making the mikoshi impressive. Zelkova is often used for such mikoshi. According to the area to be carved, different procedures are followed. For example, in the case of a torii with dragons coiling around the pillars, the gate and the dragons are carved out of one piece of wood, rather than creating the gate and the dragons separately and fixing them together.

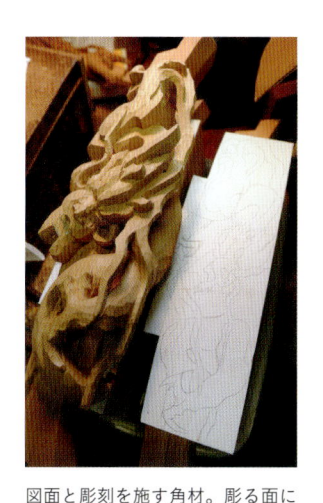

図面と彫刻を施す角材。彫る面に図面を写し立体を彫り進めていく。

A drawing and a piece of wood to be carved. The design is copied onto the wood's surface before it is carved into a 3-dimentional figure.

鳥居に巻きつく龍を彫り上げている。

A dragon crawling around the torii is being carved.

彫り上がった鳥居。笠木部分と2本の柱に龍が巻きついている。

The completed torii. Dragons are wrapped around the kasagi and the pillars.

Chapter 2: Appreciating the Design of the Mikoshi

錺(かざり)職人の伝統技法を支える工具

Tools supporting traditional metal chasing techniques

神輿の随所にはめこまれる錺金具は伝統技法によって作られ、
その工具には年季が感じられる。

Metal ornaments that beautify the mikoshi are produced by skilled artisans.
The tools speak volumes of their mastery.

錺職人の道具箱の一部。大きさも形状もさまざまなタガネが詰まっている。
A sample of metal chasers' tools. Tagane in various shapes and sizes are kept in the boxes.

鍱金具は金属の板にタガネを使って模様を打ち出す伝統技法。タガネは鋼(はがね)で作られた棒状のもので、刃がついたタガネと先端が丸いタガネの2種類に分けられるが、大きさや形は無数である。鍱職人は自分が造形したい文様のために自分でタガネを加工する。鍱職人の道具はほかに、タガネのたたくゲンノウ、金属板を切るハサミなどが多種類ある。叩く時に下に敷く台には鉄製の金床(かなとこ)やヤニ台を使う。ヤニ台は松ヤニや油脂を配合して作る軟らかいものだ。

Metal ornaments are made with a traditional technique, in which a design is formed in relief on a metal sheet by hammering from the underside with a steel chisel called a tagane. Some tagane have a blade, while others have a round edge. There are infinite types of tagane in different shapes and sizes. Some craft workers also modify their tools in order to achieve the design they want. Along with tagane, they also use hammers, special scissors to cut metal, and many other tools. The metal to be hammered is placed on an anvil or yanidai, a soft base made of a compound of resin, fat and other materials.

金属の板を切るためのハサミも形や大きさにたくさんの種類がある。

There are also various types of scissors used for cutting metal sheets.

木台と呼ばれる丸太状の台。いくつか種類の違う金床が差し込んである。

A base, looking like a tree stump, holding anvils.

写真奥にあるのが大小のゲンノウ。手前は木槌。木槌は金属の板を直接叩く用途もある。

Large and small gennou behind a wooden hammer, which is sometimes used to pound the metal plate directly.

Chapter 2: Appreciating the Design of the Mikoshi

錺金具が
神輿を豪華に荘厳に
Metal ornaments add glitz and grandeur to the mikoshi

伝統の打ち出し技術が生きる錺金具。
真鍮や銅に精緻な細工を施し金メッキで仕上げる。

With traditional metalworking skills,
elaborate reliefs appear on the brass and copper ornaments.

精巧な浮き彫りが施された錺金具。
Metal ornament with elaborate relief.

魚の卵のように小さな点で埋め尽くす魚子。
Small dots like fish roe are made by nanako carving.

錺

金具は屋根・堂・台輪のさまざまな場所に施され神輿を厳かに飾る。錺金具に使われるのは真鍮や銅の板である。まず図案を型紙にしてこれを金属板に写す。次にタガネを使って文様を彫っていく。彫り方には、文様をくり抜く「透かし彫り」・点線のような彫り跡の「蹴り彫り」・ごく細い線の「毛彫り」・魚の卵のような点状の彫りで空間を埋める「魚子」などがある。彫り上がったら周囲と表面を整え、金メッキや金箔押しで仕上げる。

Metal ornaments grace the mikoshi's august roof, dou, daiwa and many other parts. Brass and copper plates are popular materials. First, a pattern is made to copy the design onto the plate. Then the design is created on the plate with various methods. The sukashibori is a method in which patterns are cut out, while keribori makes dotted lines. Kebori, literally meaning "hair carving" draws thin lines, and nanako is used to make patterns like fish roe.

彫りつける模様のとおりに型が抜いてある(穴が空いている)型紙を金属の板につけて墨を塗ると模様が写る「墨つけ」。

The pattern is placed on the metal to copy the design on the surface with black ink.

模様の輪郭を彫る毛彫り。直線でも曲線でも自在に彫る。たんねんにタガネを当ててゲンノウで叩いていく。

The outline of the design is carved with kebori. With adept handling of the tagane and gennou, straight and curved lines are drawn on the plate.

大きめのタガネで周囲を切り離す形切り。鉄製の和式ペンチ「ヤットコ」も使う。切り離したら周囲をなめらかに仕上げる。

The completed piece is severed with larger tagane and yattoko, a sort of Japanese steel pliers. The edge of the cut-out piece is smoothened.

細工ができあがったら周囲をタガネで切り離す。

Once it is completed, the pattern is cut off along the outline with a tagane.

伝統の彩色技法で
神輿を鮮やかに

Time-honored technique makes the mikoshi colorful

日光東照宮のような極彩色を仕上げに施すことで、
神輿の木彫部分に躍動感が加わる。

Bright colors like the Nikko Toshogu Shrine
adds dynamism to wood carvings.

日本の彩色技法は古くから木彫刻とともに伝統がある。その例として最もよく知られているのは、世界遺産にもなっている日光東照宮である。木彫刻に施される彩色は神輿にも取り入れられ、白木や漆、錺金具と相まって複雑な華やかさを放っている。彩色する際に使われる絵具は、基本的には日本画の絵具と同様の岩絵具である。神輿では軒下の狛犬、唐戸、戸脇の木彫刻などに細密な彩色が施されている。

The Japanese coloring technique has as long history as that of wood carving. A prime example is the Nikko Toshogu Shrine, which has been inscribed as a World Heritage site. The same technique used to paint wood sculptures is also adopted in the coloring of mikoshi. Brilliant colors combined with a white wooden surface, a lacquered surface and metal ornaments create intricate beauty. Colorants made of ground rocks are used in Japanese painting and also for the mikoshi. Exquisite coloring can be enjoyed in the komainu under the eaves, karato, and also the carvings alongside it.

長押の狛犬はそれぞれ別の色に塗り分けられ、一つの狛犬の中にもたくさんの色が使われている。戸脇の彫刻に施された極彩色もすばらしい。

Each komainu on the nageshi is painted in many different colors. The coloring of the carvings around the doors is also brilliant.

伝統技術が
一つにまとまる組み立て

Combining traditional techniques into one mikoshi

屋根と堂をつなぐ芯柱が据えられ
すべての職人の技術が一つに組み上がる。

With the core pillar connecting the roof and the dou,
all the traditional techniques are combined into a mikoshi.a

神輿はそれぞれの木地部分が完成すると、いったん組み立てて点検をする。その後分解して漆塗り・木彫刻・錺・彩色などの工程に回る。数カ月を経てそれらの工程が終了すると、台輪の上に鳥居や囲垣を据えつけ、堂を載せ、堂の上には桝組みが載り、芯心柱を据え付け、屋根を載せて完成する。

When the major wooden parts of the mikoshi are completed, they are put together tentatively to check the whole structure, and taken apart again to finish the lacquer coating, carvings, metal ornaments and coloring, which take several months to complete. Then, the parts like the torii and igaki are attached onto the daiwa, and the dou and the masugumi are fixed. After that, the core pillar is inserted into the structure, and the roof is placed on top to complete the whole building process.

漆や錺金具が施されていない状態での仮組み。

The components are tentatively assembled without lacquer coating or decoration.

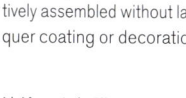

漆塗りを保護するため毛布が掛けられた屋根をクレーンで載せる。

The roof is covered with a blanket to prevent damage before placement on the structure with a crane.

各部分に木彫刻・漆・錺金具が施されて組み立て工程に集まる。 ❶

Carvings, lacquer coating and metal ornaments are applied to the components before assembling.

台輪に堂や細かい木地部分を据え最後に屋根を載せる。 ❷

The dou and small wooden parts are attached to the daiwa and the roof is placed last.

Chapter 2: Appreciating the Design of the Mikoshi　85

神輿の「粋(いき)」と「いなせ」を守る神輿師(みこしし)

The bearer of the spirit and style of mikoshi

受け継がれて来たのは伝統技術と、
それを支え次代に伝える神輿師の弛まぬ意志。

Traditional techniques and the mikoshi builders' tireless
pursuit for perfection have been passed down through generations.

神輿を製作する職人は20以上の職種に分かれる。この全体を見通して多岐にわたる仕事を受け持つ職人たちに指示を出し、それらを一つにまとめ上げるのが神輿師という仕事である。神輿師たちが目指してきたのは、祭りで人々が担ぎ、町じゅうを練り歩いた時に「粋だな」「いなせだな」と感じてもらえる神輿を作ることだと、神輿師の七代目宮本卯之助は言う。どんな神輿になるかは、最終的にすべてを決める神輿師が長い年月で培ってきた腕と経験に裏打ちされているのである。

In building the mikoshi, workers specializing in more than twenty fields of traditional arts are engaged. The mikoshi-shi, or chief builder, gives instructions to all the workers, who take on the wide-ranging tasks, and supervises the process in general. The goal of the mikoshi-shi is to create a dashing, gallant mikoshi that impresses people as it is carried around the town during the matsuri. Mikoshi-shi Miyamoto Unosuke VII maintains that the kind of mikoshi that will be created depends upon the skills and experience accumulated over a long period of time by the mikoshi-shi, who holds the ultimate responsibility.

2008(平成20)年の宮本卯之助商店の様子。神輿がある生活つまり祭りがある暮らしが、人々を元気づけ勇気づけている。

Taken at the Miyamoto Unosuke's workshop in 2008. A life with mikoshi and the matsuri keeps the people invigorated and encouraged.

第3章
Chapter 3

伝統の神輿を担ぐ

Carrying the traditional mikoshi

神輿は人が担ぐことでその目的が果たされる。
ここでは、神輿の大きさ、飾り紐の掛け方、
担ぎ棒の組み方、
神輿のじょうずな担ぎ方などを紹介する。

The mikoshi's purpose is fulfilled when it is carried by people. This chapter covers the mikoshi's size, how to attach the decorative cords, how to assemble the carrying beams, and a tip for carrying the mikoshi easily.

神輿の大きさと担ぐ人数

The size of the mikoshi and the number of bearers

大きな神輿は迫力があるが、それだけ重くなり担ぐ人数も大勢必要になる。
A large mikoshi is spectacular, but heavier, requiring more people to carry it.

延べ屋根・白木造りの子ども用神輿。錺金具や木彫刻も施してあり一見すると大人神輿と変わらない。

A white-wood mikoshi with a nobe roof for children. With metal ornaments and wood carvings, it compares favorably with those for adults.

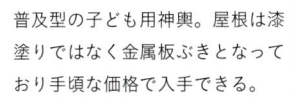

普及型の子ども用神輿。屋根は漆塗りではなく金属板ぶきとなっており手頃な価格で入手できる。

A popular type of mikoshi for children with a roof made of metal plates instead of lacquered wood. This type can be purchased for a relatively reasonable price.

神輿の大きさは、台輪の寸法（台輪の上部の一辺の長さ）で示し、それによっておおよその重さが決まってくる。一般的な台輪の寸法は１尺８寸（54㎝）から２尺３寸（69㎝）で、標準的な作りと意匠の神輿ならば１尺８寸の大きさで、担ぎ棒を含めた重さは145㎏となり、大人が担ぐ神輿としては軽量の部類になる。だが、同じ大きさでも総彫りで錺金具を多く施すとになると160㎏にもなる。標準的な神輿では、担ぎ手は何人くらいが必要になるだろう。台輪寸法が２尺（60㎝）だと、神輿に肩を入れることができる人数は約50人、これが３交代で担ぐとすると、担ぎ手は150人必要ということになる。

The size of the mikoshi is expressed by the dimension of the daiwa (the length of an upper side), which roughly determines the weight of the mikoshi. The size of a general daiwa ranges from 54 centimeters to 69 centimeters. A mikoshi with an average configuration and design measures 54 centimeters, and weighs about 145 kilograms with the carrying beams included. This is light for a mikoshi for adults, but even if the size is the same, the mikoshi's weight will increase to about 160 kilograms with carvings covering the entire surface of the wooden parts and many metal ornaments. How many people are required to carry an average mikoshi? In the case of mikoshi with a 60-centimeter daiwa, 50 people can squeeze their shoulders under the beams. Assuming the mikoshi will be carried in three shifts, 150 bearers are required.

標準的な神輿の寸法と重さ
Measurements and weight of the average mikoshi

台輪寸法 （上辺の一辺の長さ） Dimension of daiwa (the length of an above side)	最大幅 （蕨手を含む） The maximum width (including warabite)	総重量 （担ぎ棒を含む） Total weight (including the carrying beams)	担ぎの年齢層 （目安） Age groups of carriers (Estimated)
24cm（8寸）	42cm	18kg	4〜6歳　　Age 4-6
33cm（1尺1寸）	60cm	34kg	6〜8歳　　Age 6-8
39cm（1尺3寸）	71cm	58kg	9〜11歳　Age 9-11
45cm（1尺5寸）	83cm	88kg	12〜15歳／女性 Age 12-15, women
54cm（1尺8寸）	100cm	145kg	大人　　Adults
60cm（2尺）	105cm	200kg	大人　　Adults
69cm（2尺3寸）	130cm	300kg	大人　　Adults
75cm（2尺5寸）	135cm	400kg	大人　　Adults
84cm（2尺8寸）	145cm	480kg	大人　　Adults
90cm（3尺）	164cm	500kg	大人　　Adults
105cm（3尺5寸）	177cm	550kg	大人　　Adults

飾り紐の掛け方

The kazarihimo is more than just an ornament

飾り紐は装飾としてだけでなく神輿を固定する役割がある。
The decorative cords not only make the mikoshi colorful,
but also keep the components together.

❖ 飾り紐を掛ける手順　How to tie the kazarihim

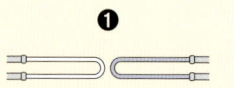

❶ 飾り紐を半分に折って長さをそろえる。
Fold the cord in half.

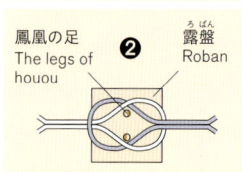

❷ 鳳凰の足／露盤 Roban／The legs of houou
鳳凰の足に飾り紐を掛けて交差させる。
Put the cord around the houou's legs and cross the ends.

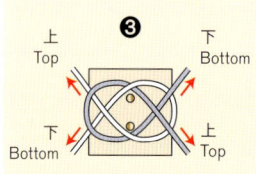

❸ 上 Top／下 Bottom／下 Bottom／上 Top
正面から見て左に来る紐が鳳凰の足元で上に交差する。
Cross the cords at the bottom of the houou with the left end on top.

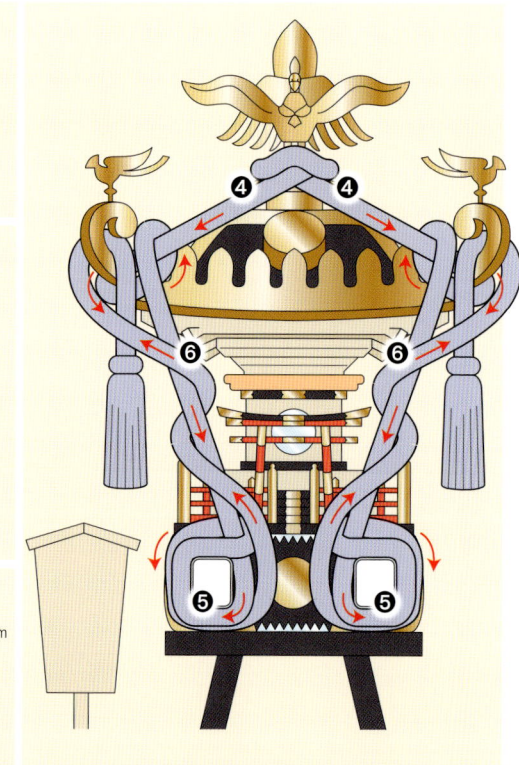

正面から見て左右それぞれに蕨手から担ぎ棒、また蕨手へと掛けていく。
Wrap each end around the warabite, coil around the carrying beam, and bring it up again and tie the ends to the warabite.

屋根の鳳凰の足下から一番下の担ぎ棒まで巻きつく飾り紐。神輿をあでやかさで飾っているが、装飾だけの目的で飾り紐がついているわけではない。伝統的な神輿には鉄くぎは使われておらず、精巧な「遊び」を持ちながら組まれている。神輿が担がれ揺り動かされた時に、飾り紐が"遊び"を生かしながら神輿全体を引き締める。白木造りの神輿には金茶色が合っているが、これは水に濡れた時に飾り紐の色落ち対策の意味もある。

The mikoshi is laced up with kazari-himo from under the houou down to the carrying beams. Colorful as it is, the kazarihimo is not just used to ornate the mikoshi. Since traditional mikoshi are meticulously assembled without using iron nails, there are slight spaces between the components. Even when the mikoshi is bouncing on people's shoulders, the kazarihimo keeps the components together, while the vibration is absorbed by the spaces. A bright gold-brown cord is often chosen for a white-wood mikoshi, not only because the colors go together, but if the mikoshi gets wet, the gold-brown cord will not make a conspicuous stain on the wood.

豪華な網掛けの飾り紐。中の紐の色は、手前が紫、左奥が金茶、右奥が水あさぎ。

Brightly colored netted kazarihimo. The one at the front is purple, the left in the back is gold-brown, and the right is pale blue.

金茶の飾り紐は白木造りの神輿に、紫の飾り紐は漆塗りの神輿に合う。

A gold-brown cord is often paired with white-wood mikoshi, while purple ones go with lacquered mikoshi.

担ぎ棒の組み方

How the carrying beams are assembled

大勢の担ぎ手を入れるために棒を増やす。

More beams are used to carry with more people

棒先金物がついた中央の2本が親棒。親棒の上で交差して神輿本体に近い位置にあるのがトンボ。トンボの外側近くで下に固定されているのが脇棒。

The two beams in the middle with metal ends are the oyabou. Tombo are laid at a right angle on the oyabou, close to the mikoshi's body. Wakibou are tied at both ends of the tombo on the underside.

親棒とトンボ、トンボと脇棒を固定する箱結び。

Hakomusubi (box knots) are used to tie oyabou and tombo, and tombo and wakibou.

神輿に多くの担ぎ手を入れるために、元からある2本の担ぎ棒を「親棒（おやぼう）」として、そこに「トンボ」や「脇棒（わきぼう）」を増やす場合も多い。親棒に対して前後それぞれに直角につけるのがトンボ、さらにトンボに対して、トンボの先端にそれぞれつけるのが脇棒だ。脇棒は、親棒から離れた位置で、親棒と平行してつく形になる。それぞれの担ぎ棒の長さは、神輿の大きさによって目安がある。台輪寸法が1尺8寸（54㎝）の神輿では、親棒は390㎝、脇棒は300㎝、トンボは180㎝になる。台輪寸法3尺（90㎝）の大きな神輿になると、親棒は630㎝、脇棒は540㎝、トンボは270㎝の長さにもなる。

In addition to the two main carrying beams, oyabou, it is common to use more shafts to carry the mikoshi with more people. The tombo ("dragonfly") are tied vertically to the oyabou, and wakibou (side beams) are attached in parallel to the oyabou at both ends of the tombo. The length of each beam is determined according to the size of the mikoshi. For a 54-centimeter daiwa, 390-centimeter oyabou, 300-centimeter wakibou, and 180-centimeter tombo are used. A larger mikoshi with a 90-centimeter daiwa needs oyabou, wakobou and tombo in lengths of 630 centimeters, 540 centimeters, and 270 centimeters, respectively.

担ぎ棒の固定に必要な麻紐や小さな板状のくさびなど。

Hemp strips and wooden wedges are also used to keep the beams fixed.

祭りをにぎやかにする
山車(だし)

Dashi adds to a matsuri's festivity

神輿と一緒に町を巡ったり、祭りの音楽を奏でる「お囃子(はやし)」が乗ったり、各地でいろいろな形がある。

Dashi floats accompany the mikoshi in the procession of the matsuri. Some floats carry musical bands, playing traditional tunes for the matsuri. There are a variety of dashi from region to region.

曳き太鼓とも呼ばれる山車。東京の下町などで戦前から最も普通に見られるタイプのもの。
The dashi topped with a drum is common in the matsuri in Tokyo's old neighborhoods.

もともと多くの祭りでは神輿は神社の宮神輿1基（まれに数基）だけで、それ以外に巡るものは、山車・曳山・鉾・屋台などと呼ばれるものだった。現在、東京の祭りでは、太鼓を載せた小型の山車（曳き太鼓）が神輿に伴うことが多い。これは、神輿を担げない小さな子どもでも祭りに参加できるようにと戦前に考案されたもので、子どもたちは山車を引っ張る綱に取りついて、太鼓を叩きながら神輿の行列と一緒に歩くことができる。

Originally, most matsuri processions consisted of a mikoshi, or occasionally a few, and various types of floats, which are called dashi, hikiyama, hoko, and yatai. Today, in most matsuri in Tokyo, the mikoshi is often accompanied by compact dashi carrying a Japanese drum. This type of dashi was invented before the war for the children not old enough to carry the mikoshi. Such children take part in the matsuri by pulling the floats forward or by playing the drums.

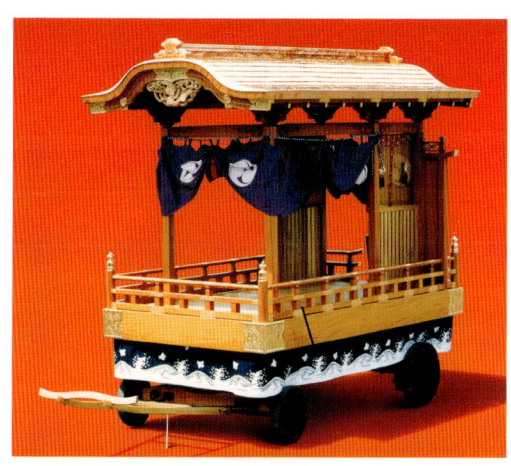

楽器を演奏するお囃子の人たちが乗る、屋台とも呼ばれる山車の一種。

The float called yatai is a vehicle for musical bands.

曳き台つきの大太鼓。巡行するよりは移動できる太鼓としての用途の意味が大きい。

This type of cart makes the drum portable, rather than serving as a festival float.

Chapter 3: Appreciating the Design of the Mikoshi

祭礼での神輿の準備

Preparing the mikoshi for the ritual

祭りの準備は伝統としきたりに従って、地域の人々が協力して行う。

People in the community make preparations for the matsuri together, following their traditions and the customs.

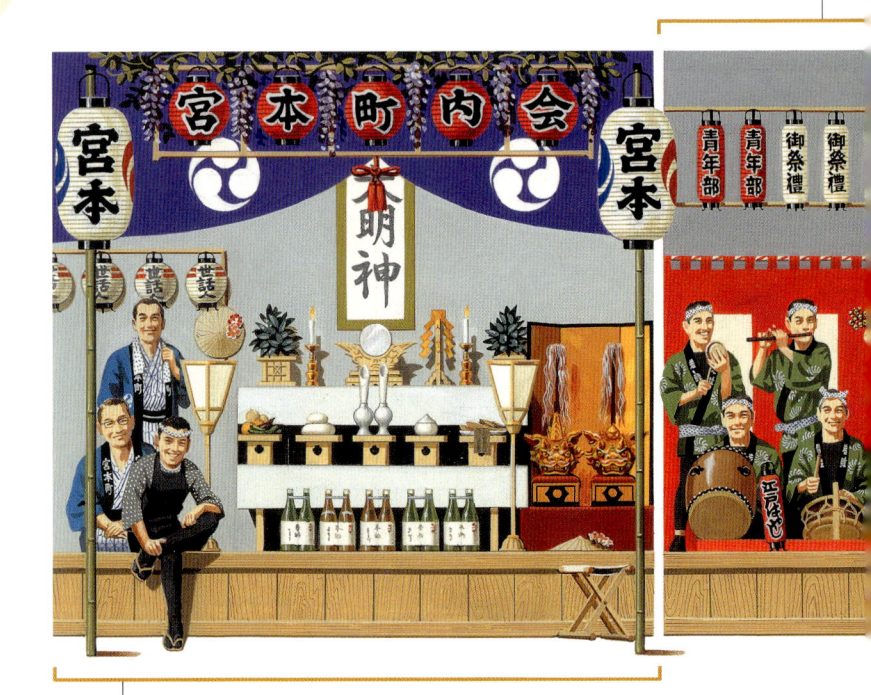

神酒所(みきしょ)

祭りの本部となる神酒所は、神社の境内や商店、空き地などに特設する。奥に祭壇をしつらえ、供物(くもつ)を上げる。ここで祭礼の指揮と管理を行い、寄付なども受けつける。座席を設けて、町内の年長者がいつでも奥に控えていられるようにする。

Mikisho

The mikisho is the festival headquarters, which is usually set up in the shrine's precincts or other places in the neighborhood such as a shop or a vacant lot. A Shinto altar is erected in the back and offerings are placed. This is where the matsuri is overseen and managed, and also where donations are received. There is also a space for elders to be seated and to stand by.

お囃子(はやし)

お囃子の場所も確保する。境内や神酒所近くのしかるべき場所に設置する。お囃子の規模や編成はその祭りによって異なる。お囃子をそっくりそのまま載せて移動できる「屋台」を使うと、神輿の渡御と一緒に移動できる。「底抜け屋台」と呼ばれる移動式の演奏台もある。

Musical players

A space for the musical band is created, normally in the shrine's precincts or near the mikisho. The scale and formation of the bands vary according to the matsuri. The players can accompany the mikoshi on a float or by using a portable stage.

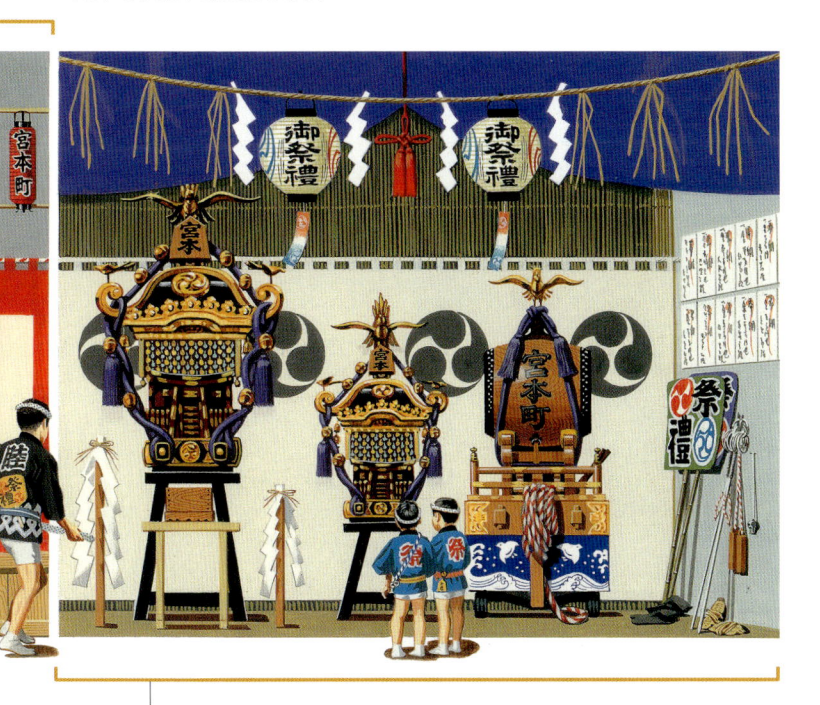

神輿の控え場所

神輿や山車は保管庫から出して控え場所に並べる。神輿は専用の休み台に載せ祭具を供える。神輿は普段はなかなか見られないので、渡御(とぎょ)(巡行＝巡り歩くこと)をしていない時にも姿を拝めるようにしておく。神輿の渡御に必要な、大うちわ、金棒(かなぼう)、拍子木(ひょうしぎ)、ホイッスルなども同じ場所に置いておく。

Mikoshi in the waiting area

Before the procession, the mikoshi and dashi are moved from the storage area to a waiting area. The mikoshi is placed on a special platform, surrounded by objects for the ritual. Since the matsuri is a special occasion when people can see the mikoshi, which is normally kept in storage, it is displayed in the waiting area for anyone to see when it is not being paraded.

Chapter 3: Appreciating the Design of the Mikoshi   97

神輿のじょうずな担ぎ方

How to carry a mikoshi

姿勢や人数などを考慮して神輿は無理なく安全に担ぐことが大切。

It is important to carry a mikoshi safely with an appropriate number of people arranged in the right positions.

神輿を安全に担ぐには、あまり猫背にならず自然な姿勢で親棒やトンボなど担ぎ棒と肩を密着させると楽だ。神輿の大きさに適した人数で担ぐことも大切で、担ぎ手の人数が集まらなかったからといって少ない人数で担ぐことはせず、同人数の交代要員も必要。神輿を担ぐ際の一つのグループは、できるだけ近い身長の人が集まると重さが分散して、担ぐリズムもとりやすい。また、神輿は台輪と担ぎ棒以外には手を触れないようにする。

To carry a mikoshi safely and easily, it is essential to maintain a natural position without curving the shoulders and to keep the beam tightly pressed against your shoulder. It is also important that the mikoshi is borne by an adequate number of people. Just because there are not enough people, the mikoshi should not be carried shorthanded. There must be enough people to take turns. To distribute the mikoshi's weight and carry it with good rhythm, it is better to group bearers of similar heights together. Be careful not to touch the mikoshi's parts aside from the daiwa and the carrying beams.

神輿で触れていいのは台輪と担ぎ棒だけ。それ以外の場所に触ると、外れてしまったりはがれてしまうことがある。

Only the daiwa and the carrying beams are the parts that can be touched. The rest of the mikoshi shoud not be touched, because the coating or ornaments might come off.

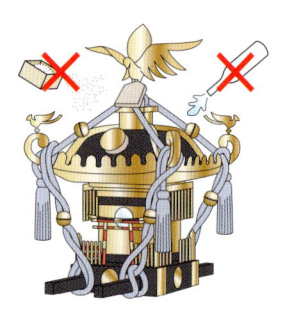

神輿には、木地、錺金具、漆などが精緻に施されているので、塩や酒をかけるとこれらが傷んでしまう。

The mikoshi consists of many delicate parts such as woodworks, metal ornaments and lacquer-coating, which can be easily damaged by salt or alcohol.

神輿を保管する方法

How to keep the mikoshi in good shape

神輿は1年に1回の数日間以外は倉庫などに保管されている。

The mikoshi is kept in storage throughout the year except for the few days of the matsuri.

数日間の祭礼に対して、それ以外は神輿は保管場所にあり次に使うのは一年後になるのが普通だ。祭礼が終わった神輿は、ていねいに手入れをして倉庫などにしまわれる。漆塗りの部分は直射日光に長く当たると、日に焼けて変色・変質してしまうことがあるので、直射日光の当たらない暗い場所が保管に適している。一方、密閉された屋内の冷暖房の効きすぎている場所はふさわしくない。

Normally, the mikoshi is used only once a year during the matsuri. After the matsuri, it must be carefully cleaned before being put back in storage. Since lacquer can be easily tarnished or altered by sunlight, it should be maintained in a dark place with no exposure to direct sunlight. A sealed, excessively air-conditioned space is not desirable either.

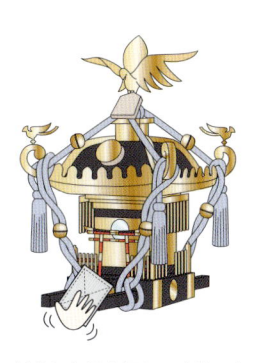

神輿に付着した汗や汚れは直後に布で拭き、しまう前にもていねいに拭く。研磨剤を使ってはいけない。

Sweat and dirt on the mikoshi must be wiped as soon as possible. Before placing it back in storage, it must be cleaned carefully without using any abrasives.

直射日光の当たらない適度の湿度がある場所が保管に適している。冷暖房が効きすぎている生活空間は適していない。

Storage with moderate humidity and no direct sunlight is ideal. An air-conditioned living space is not suited.

古くなった神輿は
修理して長く使う

Repair and maintenance for the longevity of the mikoshi

すぐれた技術で製作された神輿は修繕によって百年以上も使えるものがある。

Mikoshi built with top-notch craftworks can be used for more than a hundred years with adequate maintenance.

神輿は製作してから10〜15年ほどで、木地部分のゆるみを点検して締め直し、必要なら分解して部分品を修理したり交換したりする。さらに20〜25年を経たら全体を修理する。神輿は鉄くぎを使わない伝統技術で組み上げられているので、細部に至るまで分解することができる。部分品の交換をし、錺金具や彫刻をすべて外して磨くなどし、漆も塗り直すことで新品同様にすることができる。修理も神輿師の重要な仕事だ。

A mikoshi normally goes through an overhaul after about 10 to 15 years of use. If the wooden parts have loosened, they will be tightened back up, or taken apart and reassembled if necessary. Since the mikoshi is built with traditional techniques without using iron nails, it can be disassembled almost entirely. By replacing worn-out parts, polishing metal ornaments and wood carvings, and re-doing lacquer coatings, the mikoshi will become as good as new. Maintenance is an important part of the mikoshi-shi's job.

製作から10年以上たっていて、各部がバラバラに揺れたり、担ぎ棒にひび割れがあったり、装飾が傷んだりしている神輿は修理が必要だ。

The mikoshi needs repair work after being used for over 10 years, during which time parts become loose, cracks develop in the shafts, and ornaments get tarnished.

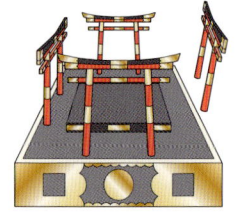

神輿はすべて分解し、欠損部分を補い、錺金具を磨き、漆塗りもすべてをはがして塗り直すことで、新品同様によみがえる。

In the overhaul, all the components are taken apart, missing parts are supplied, metal ornaments are polished, the lacquer coating is taken off and applied again, so the old mikoshi will regain the beauty and strength of a brand new one.

第 4 章
Chapter 4

神輿と祭りの歴史を探る

Learning the history of mikoshi and matsuri

日本の祭りの起源、神輿の意匠の原型である社寺建築、かつての乗り物「輿」、それに現代の祭りと神輿についてなど、神輿と祭りの歴史を解説する。

This chapter delves into the history of mikoshi and Japanese festivals, shedding light on the origin of the matsuri, the structures of temples and shrines and koshi palanquins as the models for mikoshi, as well as present-day matsuri and mikoshi.

日本の祭りの起源と
人々の祈り

The origin of matsuri and the people's prayers

日本列島に住んでいた人々は神をおそれ、
同時に身近にも感じていた。

For the people in the ancient Japanese archipelago,
the kami were awe-inspiring and yet close at the same time.

日本の祭りは有史以前から、神を人間の世界に迎えて、人々がもてなしをして、そうしてまた送り出すことを目的としていた一面がある。そこには、五穀豊穣(ごこくほうじょう)や子孫繁栄、あらゆる厄災を避けたいという原初的な願いがあり、また、祖先を敬う感謝の気持ち、さらに暮らしの変化にともなって、良縁の成就、商売繁盛、天下太平をも祈るようになった。

日本の全国各地で伝えられてきた祭りは、執り行なわれる時期、形式や様式、規模、神輿や山車などの祭具も変化に富み、大きく変容してきたものも少なくない。しかし、これらの祭りが行なわれる理由は、古代も現代も、その根底においてはそう変わってはいないといえる。

Since before the dawn of history, one of the purposes of Japanese matsuri have been to greet the kami in the human world, entertain them with feasts, and send them back to their world. What drove the people were their wishes for a good harvest, prosperity, and a life without plagues. The prayers offered to the kami were gradually combined with respect for ancestors. Also through the course of time, the people's prayers diversified, as they began to wish for a good match, success in business, and peace in the world. The matsuri that have been passed down in Japan's local regions are held at different times and in different forms, styles, and scale. The objects to be used, such as the mikoshi and dashi are also diverse. Many of the matsuri have also transformed greatly as they have been passed down through generations. But the underlying reasons these matsuri are held have not changed.

秋田県の白瀑神社の神輿は、滝壺に入って滝のしぶきを神輿ごと浴びる。山間の神社ならではの祭り。(撮影：中目雅博)

The mikoshi of the Shirataki Shrine in Akita is carried into the waterfall basin and is directly splashed. The matsuri is unique to that village in the mountains. (Photo by Masahiro Nakame)

現代に続く祭りの代表的な存在の一つ東京浅草「三社祭」。老若男女の別なく人々が担いでいる三社神輿。(撮影：阿島久夫)

The Sanja Matsuri held in Tokyo's Asakusa district is one of the major festivals of Japan today. Men, women, young and old, everybody carries the mikoshi. (Photo by Hisao Ajima)

千葉県いすみ市の「大原はだか祭り」。長い担ぎ棒を肩に載せて、上半身裸の男たちが海に入る。(撮影 武田義明)

In the Ohara Hadaka (naked) Matsuri in Isumi City, Chiba, men, stripped to the waist, carry mikoshi with extremely long beams and enter the sea. (Photo by Yoshiaki Takeda)

山梨県西八代郡の山間で見られる祭りでの神輿。若者たちが和服を着て、下駄履きで神輿を担いでいる。(撮影 森田愛三)

The matsuri in a mountainous village in Nishiyatsuhiro-gun, Yamanashi. The young men are carrying with kimono and geta sandals. (Photo by Aizou Morita)

Chapter 4: Appreciating the Design of the Mikoshi

高知県四万十市西土佐地区の祭り。
清流、四万十川に掛かる橋を祭礼の行列が渡っている。（撮影：武吉孝夫）

The matsuri of the Nishi-Tosa district in Shimanto City, Kochi. The mikoshi procession is crossing the bridge over the Shimanto River, one of the purest waterways in Japan.
(Photo by Takao Takeyoshi)

　日本の素朴な古代信仰は、やがて力を持つ人によって宗教としての体系を成すようになり、これが日本独自の宗教体系としての「神道」へと発展していく。日本で神道という言葉が初めて記されたのは720年に編まれた『日本書紀』においてである。やがて日本に伝わってきた「仏教」と神道が融合し、日本の宗教観の大きな基盤となったのである。

　日本におけるさまざまな祭りの多くは、その起源がどこにあるのか正確には分かっていない。しかし、いずれにしても非常に古い時代の庶民の素朴な信仰から生まれ、やがて権力者が司り、一方でそのまま人々の身近な生活の中に伝わり、時にそれらが離合集散した結果であろう。

The primitive worship of ancient Japan gradually gained a religious shape centering the people in power, and developed into Shinto, Japan's original systemic religion. The oldest known record regarding Shinto is found in the Nihon Shoki, the oldest book of Japanese history compiled in 720 B.C. Shinto later blended with Buddhism transferred to Japan from the Continent and became the foundation of the Japanese people's religious way of thinking.

The origins of many Japanese matsuri are not exactly known. All we know is that simple worship of the people of time immemorial has developed into the ritual presided over by those in power on one hand, while penetrating ordinary people's lives on the other, and that the formalized ritual and worship by common people played their parts in shaping the matsuri today.

山口県周南市の「貴船まつり」では、
神輿が神官とともに海を渡る珍しい様子が見られる。(撮影：和田譲)

The Kibune Matsuri of Shunan City, Yamaguchi, is an unusual matsuri in which the mikoshi is led by a Shinto priest as it proceeds through the sea. (Photo by Yuzuru Wada)

兵庫県姫路市の「灘のけんか祭り」。堂の部分を布で覆った神輿を担ぎぶつけあう勇壮な祭り。(撮影：福本いちじ)

The Nada no Kenka Matsuri (the Fighting Festival of Nada) of Himeji City, Hyogo, The mikoshi with their dou covered by a cloth clash hard against each other. (Photo by Ichiji Fukumoto)

神奈川県片瀬江ノ島で1月に行われる寒中神輿錬成大会。担ぎ手たちが波間で踏ん張っている。(撮影：冨田一雄)

The Kanchu Mikoshi Rensei Taikai is held in January in Katase-Enoshima, Kanagawa. The bearers are holding the mikoshi in the cold winter sea. (Photo by Kazuo Tomita)

神輿の原型である
神社の建築様式

The shrine architecture
as the original model of the mikoshi

神輿の造形は日本の伝統的な神社の建築様式がその原型となっている。
The mikoshi was designed with the architectural style of traditional Japanese shrines.

神社は、神道において祭祀を行う場所として、また、神がいる場所そのものとして建てられている。こうした神社建築は、日本に古くからある竪穴式住居や高床式住居に源流の一部があるとされ、さらに中国大陸や朝鮮半島からの文化も入り混じるなどして、今日見られる神社のいくつもの建築様式ができあがった。

建てられる地域や年代によって神社の様式には違いが見られるが、一般的には、神が住む場所である本殿、祭祀を行うための拝殿、神への供物を捧げる幣殿、それに鳥居、社務所、手水舎それらを取り囲む瑞垣などから構成されている。

The Shinto shrine is built as the abode of the kami and a place where rituals are presided. It is said that the architectural style of Shinto shrines partly originated from prehistoric pit dwellings and stilted houses. Mixed with cultural elements introduced from the Chinese Mainland and the Korean Peninsula, the building style we see today was established.

With some design variations depending upon the region and the time in which the structure is built, the shrine generally consists of the honden (main hall, sanctuary), which is the dwelling place of the kami, the haiden, where rituals are performed, and the heiden, a hall of offerings, as well as the torii (gates), shamucho (shrine office), chozusha (the basin where visitors purify their hands), and the mizugaki, the fences which surround all these elements.

神奈川県にある鶴岡八幡宮の建築の一部。唐破風屋根がよくわかる。

A part of the structure of the Tsurugaoka Hachimangu Shrine in Kanagawa with a karahafu roof.

神田明神の社殿。この屋根も唐破風屋根の一種である。

The structure of the Kanda Myojin Shrine. This is also a type of karahafu roof.

島根県出雲市にある出雲大社。
創建された伝承については、『古事記』や『日本書紀』にも記述が見られる。

The Izumo Taisha in Izumo City, Shimane. References to the origin of this shrine are found in the Kojiki, the oldest existing chronicle of Japan, as well as in the Nihon Shoki.

　神社の建築様式といっても、実際にはいくつもの種類がある。有名な神社で代表される様式には、出雲大社の「大社造」、住吉大社の「住吉造」、春日大社の「春日造」、伊勢神宮の「神明造」、上賀茂神社の「流造」、日吉大社の「日吉造」などがある。広島県の厳島神社は満潮になると海に浮かぶ神社となる。また、背景の山そのものが神のいる場所とされる神社もある。大きな本殿をもつ神社だけでなく街にも農村にも稲荷を祀った小さな祠は普通に見られ、ここにも神社の建築様式がある。現在は、鉄筋コンクリートで造られたり、ビルの屋上に祭られるなどさまざまだが、基本となる様式の部分は大きく変わってはいない。

京都市にある通称、下鴨神社は正式には賀茂御祖神社という。

The Kamomioya Jinja in Kyoto City is commonly known as the Shimogamo Jinja.

The shrine structures can be classified further into a number of types, and some are represented by prominent shrines. To name a few, the Taisha Style of the Izumo Taisha in Shimane, the Sumiyoshi Style of the Sumiyoshi Taisha in Osaka, the Kasuga Style of the Kasuga Taisha in Nara, the Shinmei Style of the Ise Jingu in Mie, the Nagare Style of the Kamigamo Jinja in Kyoto, and the Hiyoshi Style of the Hiyoshi Jinja in Shiga. The Itsukushima Jinja in Hiroshima Prefecture is famous for the serene image of the torii looking as though floating on the sea at high tide. Some shrines are built with the hill in the background is where the kami resides. Aside from the notable shrines with a large honden, a myriad of smaller shrines are found in towns and villages across the country, including the tiny roadside structures dedicated to the Inari, the kami of agriculture, which are also built in the same architectural style. Today, some shrines are built with reinforced concrete, while others are erected on the rooftop of a building, but the basic architectural style has not changed since olden days.

輿という乗り物と神輿の起源

Koshi and the origin of mikoshi

かつて身分の高い人が乗っていた、日本の最も古い乗り物の一つ。
One of Japan's oldest carriages used by people of eminence.

日本の最も古い乗り物の一つは、牛が引く車である「牛車（ぎっしゃ）」で、平安時代の貴族の乗り物として絵巻物（えまきもの）などにも見える。もう一つ、やはり身分の高い人たちの乗り物として人が担いで移動する輿（こし）がある。輿には担ぎ手が担ぎ棒を肩の上に載せる、より身分の高い人のための「輦輿（れんよ）」と、手をおろした状態で担ぎ棒を手に持つ「手輿（たごし）」「腰輿（ようよ）」がある。神輿と同じ担ぎ方なのは輦輿だ。輦輿でかつて天皇の乗り物とされていたのが「鳳輦（ほうれん）」で、屋根には鳳凰（ほうおう）が取りつけられ、これが神輿の形状の原型であるといえる。神輿は神の乗り物としての鳳輦であり、同時に神社を模して鳥居や階（きざはし）などが付属しているのである。

One of the oldest modes of transportation in Japan was the cattle cart called gissha, which are portrayed in old picture scrolls as the vehicle for aristocrats in the Heian Period (794 - 1192). Another means of travel for noble people was the koshi, the Japanese palanquin. Among the koshi, the renyo was a type carried on bearers' shoulders and mainly used by people of high position. The tagoshi and youyo were the palanquins which porters held by hand with their arms down. The way we carry the mikoshi is the same as that of the renyo. The renyo for the emperor was particularly called houren. The houren with its houou phoenix on the rooftop is believed the origin of the mikoshi, which as the vehicle of the kami, is also adorned with the torii and kizahashi just like a shrine.

かつての天皇の乗り物とされた鳳輦。

The houren was a carrier of the emperor.

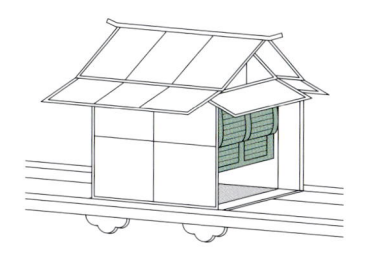

全体が白木で作られている板輿。

The itagoshi referred to the palanquins made of white wood.

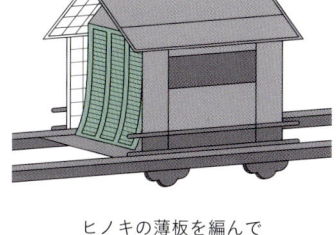

ヒノキの薄板を編んで屋根に張ってある網代輿。

The roof of the ajirogoshi is screened with nets of hinoki cypress.

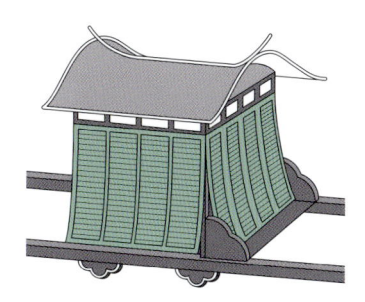

鎌倉時代から使われ唐破風屋根が載る四方輿。

The shihougoshi topped with the karahafu roof emerged in the Kamakura Period (1192 - 1333).

牛車の胴の部分の様式と似ている張輿。

The harigoshi looks similar to the body of a cattle cart.

江戸時代の
庶民の気質と祭り

The spirit of the ordinary people
in the Edo Period and the matsuri

江戸時代に花開いた文化は「江戸っ子」が作り上げた。

The Edokko culture blossomed in the Edo Period.

1603年、現在の東京都心部に江戸幕府が開かれて1867年まで続いた江戸時代には、庶民の生活も安定しその文化は現在まで続くものもある。その中心を担ったのは「江戸っ子」と呼ばれた庶民である。当時の江戸の人口は世界一であった。江戸っ子の気質は、派手好きで威勢がよく、人情味があふれたものでもあった。また、仏教と神道への信仰心は現代に比べて篤いものがあった。

　一方で、幕府（政府）は庶民に対してさまざまな制約をしており、その鬱憤を晴らすことが江戸の祭りに反映されていた。現代まで続く江戸時代の代表的な祭りは江戸三大祭りと呼ばれる「神田祭」「山王祭」「深川八幡祭」であろう。

The Edo Period began when the capital was moved to Edo, present-day Tokyo, in 1603, with that regime continuing until 1867. During this period the people enjoyed stable lives and developed a culture that has been handed down to modern times. The common people, who proudly called themselves Edokko (Edoites), were the main bearers of the culture in Edo, then the most populous town in the world. The Edokko were flamboyant, energetic and compassionate. They also had a deeper faith in Buddhism and Shinto than their modern-day counterparts. Since their lives were under various restrictions imposed by the Tokugawa Shogunate, they dispelled their gloom by applying themselves to the matsuri. The three major matsuri which have carried the tradition of the Edo culture to present day Tokyo are the Kanda Matsuri, the Sanno Matsuri, and the Fukagawa Hachiman Matsuri.

歌川広重作『名所江戸百景』から「佃しま住吉の祭」。
大きなのぼりの向こう側に、当時の神輿が描かれている。

The Sumiyoshi Matsuri on Tsukuda Island
from the One Hundred Famous Views of Edo by Ukiyoe artist, Utagawa Hiroshige.
A mikoshi of the time is portrayed behind the flag.

Chapter 4: Appreciating the Design of the Mikoshi

現代に受け継がれる
祭りと神輿

Legacy of the matsuri and the mikoshi

歴史の中で祭りと神輿は徐々に変化するが、同時に伝統も受け継がれている。
The matsuri and mikoshi have changed over the course of time, but the tradition has continued.

現代の祭りでは多くの神輿が町に繰り出すが、もともと神輿は1つの神社に1基の宮神輿（みやみこし）だけが存在し、今でも宮神輿は特別な存在である。かつて氏子たちが共有していたのは山車（だし）であった。江戸時代の祭りでは宮神輿が1基といくつかの山車があり、それが町に繰り出したのである。

江戸の祭りでは高さ数mの山車が巡行したが、19世紀の終わり頃から街に電線が張られるようになり、山車が引っ掛かる危険があったために東京では山車を巡行させるのは難しくなった。そして、山車の代わりに町神輿（まちみこし）がいくつも作られ、広まったのである。そして、地方の祭りでは現在も趣向を凝らした山車が名物となっている。

In some modern matsuri several mikoshi are brought to the street, but originally each matsuri involved only one miya-mikoshi which belonged to the shrine, while shrine parishioners owned the dashi. Even today, the miya-mikoshi is considered special. In the matsuri of the Edo Period, the people took to the street with the miya-mikoshi and several dashi floats. The dashi then were normally a few meters tall. Since using dashi in parades became difficult in Tokyo as overhead electric cables were installed at the end of the 19th century, neighborhood associations' machi-mikoshi (town mikoshi) gradually increased in number and took over the floats. Dashi, however, remain as main attractions in a number of regional matsuri with various original features.

時代と場所ははっきりと分からないが、
1930年代の戦争前か戦後間もない頃の祭りでの集合写真。(宮本卯之助商店所蔵)

A group photo during the matsuri. Time and place are unknown, but estimated to have been taken in the 1930s or shortly after the Second World War. (From the Miyamoto Unosuke Shoten's archive)

現代の三社祭の様子。戦前はもちろん江戸時代、明治時代の頃の様子も、そう変わりはなかったかも知れない。(撮影：兼坂正造)

The Sanja Matsuri today. The basic elements of the matsuri do not seem to have changed so much since the pre-war era, or even the Meiji and Edo Periods. (Photo by Shozo Kanesaka)

戦前であろうか東京での祭りの様子。着物を着た大人たちが神輿を担ぎ、周囲で子どもや女性が見守っている。(宮本卯之助商店所蔵)

A photo of a matsuri in Tokyo, seemingly taken before the war. Men in kimono carry the mikoshi, while women and children watch. (From the Miyamoto Unosuke Shoten's archive)

Chapter 4: Appreciating the Design of the Mikoshi

湯島天神大祭での神輿。神輿の屋根には天神のシンボルである梅の紋が見える。（撮影 青木茂）

The mikoshi in the Yushima Tenjin Annual Festival. On the roof is the crest of the plum flower, the symbol of the shrine. (Photo by Shigeru Aoki)

　1930年代に中国との戦争が始まると人々の生活は徐々に余裕を失い、1941年にはアメリカ・イギリスなどとの戦争が始まり、東京など都市では空襲によって多くの命や財産そして神輿も失われた。しかし、1945年に戦争が終わると人々は祭りを求め、1948年には東京の浅草で三社祭が復活した。1950年から1960年頃までは神輿を新調する大ブームが起こり、年間で200基を作った製作所もあった。1960年代以降は高度経済成長の中で娯楽が多様化し、地域の様子も変わった。それに伴って新しいコミュニティが祭りを担うようになった。一方で古くからの祭りの伝統も残り、新しい世代が受け継ぐ動きもある。

As Japan engaged in war with China in the 1930s, the people's lives were put under a harsh environment. With the outbreak of war with the United States and Great Britain in 1941, massive air raids targetting Tokyo and other large cities destroyed millions of lives along with their property, as well as the mikoshi. When the war came to an end in 1945, the people sought diversion in the matsuri, and the Sanja Matsuri in Tokyo's Asakusa district was resumed in 1948. The period from the 1950s to the 1960s saw a mikoshi construction boom, with some makers producing as many as 200 in a year. As the high economic growth diversified the people's entertainment choices in the 1960s, the way of local communities also changed. Some matsuri are now led by newly formed communities, while others have maintained their tradition through generations.

深川八幡の通称「水掛け祭り」。真夏の炎天下、人も神輿もじゃぶじゃぶと水をかぶっている。（撮影 石川心一）

The Fukagawa Hachiman Shrine's matsuri, commonly known as the "water-splashing festival." In the heat of the summer, the bearers and the mikoshi are showered with plentiful amounts of purifying water.

農村での春の祭りの風景。山や田植え前のあぜ道を行く神輿が晴れやかに見える。大きく立派な神輿である。（撮影 森田愛三）

A farming village's matsuri. The large, magnificent mikoshi is shining against the background of mountains and rice paddies before planting. (Photo by Aizo Morita)

Chapter 4: Appreciating the Design of the Mikoshi

神輿作りの伝統技術と変遷

Traditional mikoshi-building techniques and transitions

現代の神輿作りには最新技術と伝統技術の両方が生かされている。
The latest and time-honored techniques are combined in the mikoshi-building of today.

神輿を作るための技術は古い時代に既に非常な進歩を遂げたが、現代になって大工道具をはじめとして電動工具が使われるようになり、効率化が進んだ。運搬手段の発達も著しく、材料となる木材を伐採地から神輿の製作所まで運ぶ時間や労力も、戦前に比べて格段に短縮され軽減された。顧客とのやり取りも、IT化によって早く正確になった。しかし、神輿作りの現場では、昔からの大工道具も数多く使い続けられている。それは、手作業によってしか出せない繊細さや美しさがあるからだ。そして、神輿が作られ続けることで、これらの技術もまた伝え続けられる。

The techniques of mikoshi builders in old days were already highly sophisticated. In recent years, however, more and more electronic tools have been introduced to the building of structures, along with improved efficiency. Also, thanks to the remarkable improvement in the methods of transportation, the time required to transfer lumber from logging areas to the workshop has been extremely shortened, and has enabled quick, accurate communication with clients. But in building the mikoshi, a host of old-fashioned carpenter tools are still playing irreplaceable roles, because there are subtle expressions that can only be achieved by skilled handiwork. As long as the mikoshi continue to be built, traditional craftsmanship will stay alive.

1924年頃の宮本卯之助商店。（宮本卯之助商店所蔵）

A photo of the Miyamoto Unosuke Shoten around 1924.
(From the Miyamoto Unosuke Shoten's archive)

1933年頃の宮本卯之助商店。（宮本卯之助商店所蔵）

A photo of the Miyamoto Unosuke Shoten around 1933.
(From the Miyamoto Unosuke Shoten's archive)

Chapter 4: Appreciating the Design of the Mikoshi 119

今こそ日本中で祭りを

Promoting the matsuri nationwide

祭りは日々の安全を祈り生活に潤いを与え世代間に交流をもたらす。

The matsuri represents people's prayers, enriches their lives, and enhances cross-generation exchange

神事としての祭りは、土地の神を崇めることで日々の生活の安全を感謝し、安心を願うことに意味がある。一方で、非日常の楽しみとしての祭りには、盛装し歌ったり踊ったり大きな声を出すことで、日頃の鬱憤を吐き出して明日への英気を養う目的がある。また、地域の中で世代間をつなげる役割も果たす。地域社会のつながりが薄くなり、核家族化が進行する中で、祭りが現代人の生活で果たす新たな役割も注目され始めている。

The meaning of the matsuri as a Shinto ritual is to worship the local kami and to give thanks for everyday lives with no mishaps. In the matsuri as an extraordinary circumstance of festivity, the people vent daily stress by donning special consumes, singing, dancing, and shouting to restore their energy to get back to their normal lives. The matsuri's additional role is to connect people in the neighborhood. As community ties become weaker and the proportion of nuclear households rises, the role played by the matsuri in modern Japan is being reevaluated.

1954年頃の宮本卯之助商店。大きな看板に描かれた神輿と太鼓、店の前には神輿製作を依頼したと思われる関係者が揃っている。（宮本卯之助商店所蔵）

A photo taken around 1954 shows the Miyamoto Unosuke Shoten with large billboards of mikoshi and a drum. Some of the people are thought to be clients who commissioned the building of the mikoshi. (From the Miyamoto Unosuke Shoten's archive)

第 5 章
Chapter 5

全国の祭りを旅する

Exploring Japan's regional matsuri

大きな山車や曳山が登場する祭り、伝統の上に新しい感覚が加わった祭りなど、日本にはさまざまな祭りがある。全国の21の祭りを紹介する。

With overwhelming dashi and hikiyama and modern elements combined with tradition, each of Japan's regional matsuri showcases unique, fascinating features. This chapter introduces twenty-one of these matsuri.

青森ねぶた祭
Aomori Nebuta Matsuri

開催時期・期間：毎年8月2～7日　規模：およそ300万人　開催場所：青森県青森市

Dates: August 2 - 7, held annually　**Estimated number of spectators:** 3,000,000
Place: Aomori City, Aomori Prefecture

各地で見られる七夕祭りでの灯籠流しが、この地方で独自に変化したものといわれる。巨大な灯籠である「ねぶた」は台車部分を含めて最大幅9m、奥行き7m、高さ5mで重さは4tにもなる。ねぶたは「ねぶた師」が3カ月ほどかけて製作する。ハネト（踊り手）は1台のねぶたに500～1000人ほどがついて踊り、期間を通じては9万人ものハネトが参加するという。1980年に国の重要無形民俗文化財に指定されている。

The Nebuta Matsuri originates from the toro nagashi, a ceremony to release lanterns in the river to guide the spirits of the departed to their world, The toro nagashi, while being held in many parts of Japan, has developed an original form in Aomori. Giant paper lanterns, nebuta, are nine meters at their widest part, seven meters in depth, five meters in height, and weighing as much as four tons. It takes special craft workers about three months to complete the nebuta. In the parade, each nebuta is accompanied by anywhere from 500 to 1,000 dancers, haneto. As many as 90,000 haneto are said to take part in the matsuri during the period. The matsuri was designated as a significant intangible folk cultural asset of Japan in 1980.

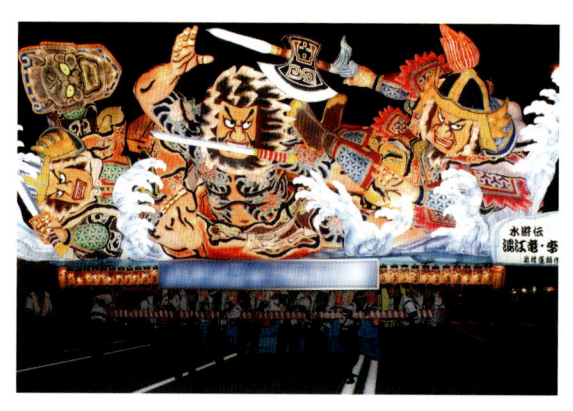

【青森ねぶた祭オフィシャルサイト】
Aomori Nebuta Matsuri official website
- http://www.nebuta.or.jp/
- http://www.atca.info/nebuta_en/

豪壮な「ねぶた」が巡幸しハネトが踊り、祭りの音楽「囃子」が鳴り渡る。

Spectacular parade of nebuta and haneto dancers go around the town accompanied by traditional festival music, hayashi.

弘前ねぷたまつり
Hirosaki Neputa Matsuri

開催時期・期間：毎年8月1日～7日　　規模：およそ160万人　　開催場所：青森県弘前市

Dates: August 1 - 7, annual　　**Estimated number of spectators:** 1,600,000
Place: Hirosaki City, Aomori Prefecture

弘前ねぷたまつりには、扇形の「扇ねぷた」と人形型の「組みねぷた」の2種類が登場する。ねぷたの運行は、最初に団体名を記した前灯籠や町印、小型の前ねぷた、ねぷたの綱を引く曳き手、大型のねぷた、囃子方と続く。大型のねぷたは、市街地の電線や看板に引っかからないように、それらを見事にかわしながら止まることなく進む。掛け声は独特のもので「ヤーヤドー」という。1980年に国の重要無形民俗文化財に指定された。

The giant lanterns here are called the neputa, which can be classified into two types: the ohgi neputa shaped like a folding fan, and the human-shaped kumi neputa. The parade is led by lanterns signaling the names of organizations and neighborhood associations, followed by small-sized neputa, then the large neputa is pulled forward on ropes, with musical bands. Large neputa are skillfully navigated so as not to hit overhead electric cables and signs, with unique shouts that go, "Yah, ya, doh!" The matsuri was designated as a significant intangible folk cultural asset of Japan in 1980.

【弘前市観光コンベンション協会】
Hirosaki Tourism and Convention Bureau
- http://www.hirosaki-kanko.or.jp/web/index.html
- http://www.hirosaki-kanko.or.jp/en/

扇ねぷたの表側を飾る「鏡絵」には武者絵などが描かれている。

Colorful paintings of samurai warriors grace the front side of the ohgi neputa.

角館のお祭り
かくのだて

The Festivals of Kakunodate

開催時期・期間：毎年9月7〜9日　**規模**：およそ20万人　**開催場所**：秋田県仙北市

Dates: September 7 - 9, held annually　**Estimated number of spectators:** 200,000
Place: Senboku City, Akita Prefecture

巡行するいくつも曳山が登場し、町の数カ所には人形を飾った「置山(おきやま)」が置かれる。曳山は参拝からの帰りの「下り山(くだりやま)」と、これから向かう「上り山(のぼりやま)」が路上で鉢合わせするが「上り山」に通行の優先権があるとされている。下り山同士の場合は交渉をするが、決裂すると"実力"で通るための「やまぶっつけ」になる。やまぶっつけは、現在では観光として決まった場所と時間で見られる。祭りは国の重要無形民俗文化財に指定されている。

【仙北市観光情報】
Semboku City Sightseeing Information

- http://www.city.semboku.akita.jp/sightseeing/index.html
- http://www.city.semboku.akita.jp/en/index.html

This festival exhibits a number of floats, the hikiyama, and the okiyama, which are set up at several sites in the town. When a hikiyama proceeding to the shrine runs into another hikiyama coming back from the shrine, the one heading for the shrine has the right to pass and the other has to give way. In the event two hikiyama meet on their way from the shrine, the two groups decide which goes first through negotiation. If the negotiation breaks off, the dispute will be settled by force with the yama-buttuke, in which the two floats are banged against each other. Today, the yama-buttuke is demonstrated for tourists at certain times and places during the period. The matsuri has been designated as a significant intangible folk cultural asset of Japan.

曳山同士が立ち上がるようにして激突する「やまぶっつけ」。

The two hikiyama ram into each other in the yama-buttuke

仙台・青葉まつり
Sendai Aoba Matsuri

開催時期・期間：毎年5月第3日曜日とその前日　規模：およそ93万人　開催場所：宮城県仙台市

Dates: the third Sunday of May and the eve, held annually　**Estimated number of spectators**: 930,000
Place: Sendai City, Miyagi Prefecture

豪華絢爛な11基の仙台山鉾が、青葉神社の神輿渡御、甲冑武者の行列に続く。山鉾は高さ6m、重さは6tから8tもあり、それぞれに安全祈願、商売繁盛、家内安全などの人々の願いが込められている。また、軽快なお囃子の演奏に合わせて約4000人が演舞する「すずめ踊り」も圧巻だ。17世紀中頃が起源だといわれているが、1960年頃にいったん途絶えてしまった。それが1985年に復活し、今では東北三大祭りの一つと数えられる。

【仙台・青葉まつり協賛会】
Sendai Aoba Matsuri Sponsor Association
- http://www.aoba-matsuri.com/index.html

The matsuri boasts eleven magnificent floats, yamahoko, led by the mikoshi of the Aoba Shrine as well as a procession of armor-clad samurai warriors. Each of the yamahoko, about six meters in height, weighing from six to eight tons, represent the locals' prayers for tranquil lives, success in business and safety for their families. Another attraction is the Suzume Odori (sparrow dance), a rhythmical performance by as many as 4,000 dancers. The Suzume Odori, believed to have begun in the middle of the 17th century, ceased once in the 1960s and was resumed in 1985. The Aoba Matsuri is known as one of the three major festivals of the Tohoku (northeastern) region.

人々は山鉾を囲みすずめ踊りで舞い祭りを活気づける。

The enlivening Suzume Odori dancers surround the floats.

二本松ちょうちん祭り
Nihonmatsu Chochin Matsuri

開催時期・期間： 毎年10月4〜6日　**規模：** およそ18万人　**開催場所：** 福島県二本松市

Dates: October 4 - 6, held annually　**Estimated number of spectators:** 180,000
Place: Nihonmatsu City, Fukushima Prefecture

祭りでは提灯で飾られた約11mの高さの太鼓台が登場する。太鼓台1基に提灯は300個以上が吊るされており、夜には神事に従ってかがり火から提灯のろうそくに火が移される。太鼓台は7つある地域の町から各1基ずつが出揃う。大きな太鼓台が方向転換する時の方法や掛け声、お囃子は7つの町内それぞれに特徴がある。1基の太鼓台で消費されるろうそくは1晩で1500本を越し、このろうそくを取り替える若者たちの手際も見どころだ。

The main attraction of the Chochin Matsuri is the eleven-meter-tall floats, taikodai, with more than three hundred chochin (paper lanterns). After sundown, the Shinto ritual of lighting the candles with the flame from a bonfire is conducted. Each of the seven communities produces a taikodai and they have individual methods, shouts and chants used when the huge taikodai turns around a corner. More than 1,500 candles are consumed by each float per night, and the way the local youth skillfully replace them is also interesting to watch.

【二本松市観光ガイド】
Nihonmatsu City Sightseeing Guide website
- http://www.city.nihonmatsu.lg.jp/site/kankou/

提灯に火が入る頃に祭りは最高潮を迎える。

The matsuri culminates around the time the lanterns are lit.

秩父神社例大祭
Chichibu Shrine Annual Festival

開催時期・期間：毎年12月2〜3日　　規模：およそ25万人　　開催場所：埼玉県秩父市

Dates: December 2 - 3, held annually　　**Estimated number of spectators:** 250,000
Place: Chichibu City, Saitama Prefecture

祭りの最大の見どころは、豪華な彫刻が施された大きな笠鉾と屋台だ。勇壮な屋台太鼓が打ち鳴らされ、2基の笠鉾と4基の屋台が引き回される。屋台の上では「秩父歌舞伎」や「曳き踊り」が上演される。これらの笠鉾や屋台はすべて国の重要文化財に指定され、歌舞伎なども国の重要無形民俗文化財である。引き回される笠鉾や屋台の方向転換も見事で、進行を取り仕切る者の手さばきであざやかに町の辻を曲がって進んで行く。

The highlight of the festival is the lavishly sculptured floats called kasahoko and the yatai. Amid the powerful sound of the drums, two kasahoko and four yatai are pulled around the town. The yatai also serve as the stage of theatrical drama, the Chichibu Kabuki, and dance performance, Hikiodori. All the kasahoko and yatai are designated as national important cultural properties, while the Chichibu Kabuki is a significant intangible folk cultural asset. The way the massive floats are pulled by skilled hands and make sharp turns is fascinating.

【秩父観光協会】
Chichibu Tourism Association
● http://www.chichibuji.gr.jp

見事な手さばきによって笠鉾や屋台が豪快に辻を曲がる

The way the enormous kasahoko and yatai are pulled around corners is a remarkable feat.

Chapter 5: Appreciating the Design of the Mikoshi

八坂祭典熊谷うちわ祭

Yasaka Saiten Kumagaya Uchiwa Matsuri

開催時期・期間：毎年7月20〜22日　規模：およそ70万人　開催場所：埼玉県熊谷市

Dates: July 20 - 22, held annually　**Estimated number of spectators:** 700,000
Place: Kumagaya City, Saitama Prefecture

16世紀頃がこの祭りの起源とされ、20世紀の初め頃にうちわを配るようになったことから「うちわ祭」と呼ばれるようになった。3日間の祭りでは、華やかに飾られた全部で12基の山車と屋台が町のあちこちを巡行する。ここでのお囃子は大きな鉦を打ち鳴らすことが特徴で、この鉦と太鼓の音が合わさって勇壮な「熊谷囃子」の演奏となる。祭りの最終日の夜には、これらの山車・屋台が集まってお囃子を競い合う「叩き合い」が行なわれる。

The matsuri, believed to have originated in the 16th century, came to be known as the Uchiwa Matsuri as uchiwa (paper fans) began to be handed out to spectators around the beginning of the 20th century. The twelve dashi, all brilliantly decorated, and yatai parade around each corner of the town. The music played in this matsuri, known as the Kumagaya Bayashi, is characterized by the sound of large gongs, which mingles with strong drum beats. The finale of the matsuri is the tatakiai, in which all the dashi and yatai gather and boisterously compete accompanied by hayashi music.

【熊谷うちわ祭公式ホームページ】
Kumagaya Uchiwa Matsuri official website
- http://uchiwamatsuri.com/

山車・屋台で鉦と太鼓を打ち鳴らす「叩き合い」が大きな魅力。

The lively performance of gongs and drums in the tatakiai is a major attraction.

桐生八木節まつり
Kiryu Yagibushi Matsuri

開催時期・期間：毎年8月の第1金〜日曜日　　規模：およそ45万人　　開催場所：群馬県桐生市

Dates: from Friday to Sunday of the first week of August, held annually
Estimated number of spectators: 450,000　　**Place:** Kiryu City, Gunma Prefecture

歴史的な「桐生祇園祭」と郷土芸能である「八木節」の2つが祭りの柱になっている。祭りには高さ約9mの「鉾」と歴史的な価値の高い「屋台」が登場する。鉾の巡行は一時途絶えていたものが近年になって復活した。屋台には豪華な絵がはめ込まれており「動く祭礼建築物」ともいわれる。これら鉾や屋台の巡行に加えて、昔ながらの郷土芸能としての八木節の演奏と踊り、現代風にアレンジされたダンス八木節なども見ることができる。

The historical festival, Kiryu Gion Matsuri, and the local performing art, Yagibushi, are the two pillars of the Kiryu Yagibushi Festival, which involves two types of floats: the nine-meter-tall hoko and historically valuable yatai. The parade of the hoko was recently revived after decades of hiatus. The yatai with gorgeous art works on the surface are dubbed "moving festival architecture." Along with the procession of the hoko and yatai, the people also enjoy the Yagibushi music and dance, including a version that has been rearranged to more modern tastes.

【桐生八木節まつりオフィシャルサイト】
Kiryu Yagibushi Festival official website
- http://kiryu-matsuri.net/index.html

人々は輪になりながら八木節を踊る。
People perform the Yagibushi dance in circles.

Chapter 5: Appreciating the Design of the Mikoshi

三社祭
さんじゃまつり

Sanja Matsuri

開催時期・期間: 毎年5月の第3週目の金土日　**規模:** およそ150万人　**開催場所:** 東京都台東区

Dates: From Friday to Sunday of the third week of May, held annually
Estimated number of spectators: 1,500,000　**Place:** Taito Ward, Tokyo

祭りの1日目には、歴史的な衣装の人たちが、伝統的な祭りの音楽である囃子に乗って練り歩く「大行列」がある。2日目には、地域の44の町神輿が集合して浅草神社でお祓いを受けたあとに、順番に町に出て練り歩く「町内神輿連合渡御」が行なわれる。すべての神輿を送り出すのに3時間もかかるといわれている。そして3日目に、本社神輿が地域の町内を巡る。この祭りで三社型のさまざまな神輿を多数見ることができる。

The Sanja Matsuri opens with the grand parade by people in historical attire, marching to traditional hayashi music. On the second day, the mikoshi from forty-four neighborhoods are purified at the Asakusa Shrine and appear on the streets one after another. It takes nearly three hours for all the mikoshi to be released. The procession of the shrine's own three Honja Mikoshi is reserved for the final day. The Sanja Matsuri offers a golden opportunity to appreciate various sanja-style mikoshi.

【浅草神社奉賛会 三社祭 公式サイト】
Asakusa Shrine Supporters' Association Sanja Matsuri official website
- http://www.sanjasama.jp

神社から順番に神輿が出発する。
Mikoshi leave the shrine one after another.

山王祭
Sanoh Matsuri

開催時期・期間：神幸祭は2年に1度 6月7〜17日　規模：およそ45万人　開催場所：東京都千代田区

Dates (the Shinkosai)**:** June 7 - 17, held biennially　**Estimated number of spectators:** 450,000
Place: Chiyoda Ward, Tokyo

江戸時代の歴代将軍が見る「天下祭」が起源。山王祭の最大の儀式は「神幸祭」で、御鳳輦と呼ばれる輿が2基、宮神輿1基、山車3基、それに古代の王朝の衣服を着た人々が列をなして巡行する。その人数は総勢500人ともいわれ、300mの長さで東京駅前や銀座を練り歩く。また、日枝神社の氏子（土地の神社の信者）による山車と神輿の渡御、子どもたちの「稚児行列」も見どころだ。大掛かりな「神幸祭」は西暦の偶数年に行なわれる。

Originating from the Tenka Matsuri, which was offered to the Shogun during the Edo Period, the matsuri's largest event is the Shinkosai parade, featuring two gohouren (the emperor's palanquin), the miya-mikoshi, three dashi floats, as well as almost 500 people dressed in ancient dynastic costumes. The 300-meter-long parade passes in front of Tokyo Station and the Ginza district. Equally spectacular is the procession of the dashi and the mikoshi by the Hie Shrine parishioners and children's parade, Chigo Gyoretsu. The grand Shinkosai parade is held only in even-numbered years.

【日枝神社山王祭オフィシャルサイト】
Hie Jinja Sanoh Matsuri official site
- http://www.hiejinja.net/jinja/sanoh/

東京・銀座四丁目交差点を巡行する御鳳輦。

The gohouren passes an intersection of the posh Ginza district.

Chapter 5: Appreciating the Design of the Mikoshi

富岡八幡宮例祭
Tomioka Hachimangu Reisai

開催時期・期間：本祭りは3年に1度 8月15日前後　　規模：およそ30万人　　開催場所：東京都江東区

Dates: Around August 15th, held triennially　　**Estimated number of spectators:** 300,000
Place: Koto Ward, Tokyo

「深川八幡祭り」とも呼ばれ、3年に1度の本祭りでは大小合わせて120基以上の町神輿が担がれる。そのうちの大神輿54基による「神輿連合渡御」は、伝統的な歌や踊りに続き、道で演奏される囃子の中で早朝から夕刻まで列をなして練り歩く。担ぎ手の掛け声は伝統的な「ワッショイワッショイ」である。沿道からは「清めの水」が絶えず掛けられることから「水掛け祭り」の異名もあり、盛夏の中、担ぎ手も観衆も水に濡れて盛り上がる。

【富岡八幡宮深川八幡祭り】
Tomioka Hachimangu Shrine
Fukagawa Hachiman Matsuri

- http://www.tomiokahachimangu.or.jp/htmls/maturih1.html

The regular festival of the Tomioka Hachimangu Shrine, commonly known as the Fukagawa Hachiman Matsuri, is held every three years with more than 120 large and small machi-mikoshi taking to the streets. Large mikoshi also appear in the grand joint procession, the Mikoshi Rengo Togyo. Following the performance of traditional song and dance, fifty-four enormous mikoshi crisscross the town from early morning till evening to the hayashi music played in the streets and the familiar shouts by mikoshi bearers, "Wasshoi, wasshoi." The unique feature of this matsuri is the purifying water thrown on the procession by spectators, hence its nickname, the Mizukake Matsuri (water-splashing festival). In the height of the summer heat both bearers and spectators get doused and together pump up the excitement of the matsuri.

神輿の担ぎ手たちに絶えず水が掛けられる。

The bearers are constantly showered with purifying water.

神田祭
Kanda Matsuri

開催時期・期間：大祭は2年に1度 5月中旬の土日　　規模：およそ30万人　　開催場所：東京都千代田区

Dates (the Taisai): A weekend in the middle of May, held biennially
Estimated number of spectators: 300,000　　**Place:** Chiyoda Ward, Tokyo

神田祭は山王祭と同じく江戸時代の将軍が見る天下祭であり、山王祭と対をなしてそれぞれの大祭は隔年毎に交互に行なわれる。見どころは「神幸祭」で、鳳輦・神輿を先頭にしたにぎやかな行列「附け祭」が練り歩く。附け祭には山車や騎馬武者などが続くが、近年では現代的なものも増え、氏子の地域に秋葉原が含まれていることから、アニメのキャラクターをかたどったバルーンなども登場する。夕方には100基の神輿が神田明神に繰り込む。

Along with the Sanoh Matsuri, the Kanda Matsuri was used as the festival for the Shogun during the Edo Period. The key events of the Sanoh Matsuri and the Kanda Matsuri are held every other year in turns. The highlight of the Kanda Matsuri is the Shinkosai, in which the houren and mikoshi lead the joyous parade, Tuke Matsuri, composed of dashi floats and mounted samurai. Recently, modern motifs are also seen in the parade. Since the shrine's parishioner areas include the Akihabara district, balloons of anime characters also join the parade. In the evening, as many as a hundred mikoshi gather at the Kanda Myojin Shrine.

【神田明神サイト】
Kanda Myojin website
- http://www.kandamyoujin.or.jp

江戸三大祭りに数えられる神田明神の祭り。

Kanda Myojin's matsuri is one of Tokyo's three major festivals.

Chapter 5: Appreciating the Design of the Mikoshi

茅ヶ崎海岸浜降祭

Chigasaki Kaigan Hamaorisai

開催時期・期間：7月の第3月曜日（海の日）　規模：およそ8万人　開催場所：神奈川県茅ヶ崎市

Dates: the third Monday of July (the Marine Day)　**Estimated number of spectators:** 80,000
Place: Chigasaki City, Kanagawa Prefecture

　この祭りの始まりは19世紀の初め頃で、寒川神社への信仰と、海で「禊」をすることが起源だと言われている。禊とは、神事に際して水を浴びるなどして罪や体を清めること。見どころは、神輿が浜に降りて潮風を受け禊を行なう姿で、いくつかの神輿は海へ入って行く。祭りの日の早朝には青竹と幟が高々と浜に掲げられ、茅ヶ崎市と寒川町から40基の神輿が集まる。神官に祈祷をしてもらったあと、神輿は担ぎ手と共に海に入る。

The origin of this Hamaorisai (the beach-descending festival) is believed to be the misogi in the sea by the worshipers of the Samukawa Shrine in the beginning of the 19th century. The misogi is the practice of purifying one's body in water before a Shinto ritual. The main attraction of this matsuri is the mikoshi's beachside purification in sea winds. Some mikoshi also enter the water. In early morning, bamboo poles and flags start rising on the beach, where forty mikoshi will arrive from around Chigasaki City and Samukawa Town. After the prayers by Shinto priests, the mikoshi are carried into the sea one after another.

【茅ヶ崎市観光・イベント】
Chigasaki City sightseeing and event information
- http://www.city.chigasaki.kanagawa.jp/kankou.html
- http://www.city.chigasaki.kanagawa.jp.e.ox.hp.transer.com/kankou.html

富士山を背景に神輿が海に入って行く。

The mikoshi enter the sea against the background of Mt. Fuji.

高岡御車山祭
Takaoka Mikurumayama Matsuri

開催時期・期間：毎年5月1日　規模：およそ14万人　開催場所：富山県高岡市

Dates: May 1st, held annually　**Estimated number of spectators:** 140,000
Place: Takaoka City, Toyama Prefecture

この祭りは、1588年に豊臣秀吉が天皇をお迎えする際に使った御所車が起源とされる。やがて江戸時代の名工たちによって豪華な7基の御車山として揃えられ、高岡関野神社の祭礼として400年以上を経た今日も町を巡行している。御車山には伝統的な服装の氏子たちがつき従い、男の子が乗り込んで古風な囃子を演奏する。御車山はそれぞれに装飾が異なっているが、どれもすぐれた工芸技術が施され、国の重要文化財にも指定されている。

【高岡御車山保存会公式サイト】
Takaoka Mikurumayama Preservation Association
- http://mikurumayama.jp

This matsuri was originally dedicated to the emperor's carriage which he used to visit the feudal lord Toyotomi Hideyoshi at his Kyoto palace in 1588. Later in the Edo Period (1603 - 1868), seven more lavish floats were built by prominent craftsmen. After 400 years the floats are still being used in the parade of the Takaoka Sekino Shrine's festival. The floats, called the mikurumayama (emperor's carriage), are accompanied by parishioners dressed in traditional costumes, while boys perform hayashi music on the floats. The mikurumayama, each decorated in different tastes but with equally excellent craftworks, are designated as national important cultural properties.

伝統的な衣装を着た氏子たち。

Shrine parishioners clad in traditional garb.

Chapter 5: Appreciating the Design of the Mikoshi

浜松まつり
Hamamatsu Matsuri

開催時期・期間：毎年5月3〜5日　規模：およそ150万人　開催場所：静岡県浜松市

Dates: May 3 - 5, held annually　**Estimated number of spectators:** 1,500,000
Place: Hamamatsu City, Shizuoka Prefecture

この祭りは神社や寺の祭礼とは異なり、都市祭りといわれる市民の祭りである。起源は、一説によると16世紀中頃にこの地方を統治していた領主の長男誕生を祝って凧を揚げたこととされる。見どころは昼間に行なわれる「凧揚げ合戦」と夜に行なわれる「御殿屋台引き回し」。83台の御殿屋台が市中心部を巡行し、屋台にはお囃子が乗る。ここで演奏されるお囃子は、多くの祭りで奏されるお囃子とは違う歌舞伎囃子と呼ばれる独特のものだ。

Unlike the matsuri associated with shrines and temples, the Hamamatsu Matsuri is a citizen-led festival. One theory holds that the festival began when a local lord flew kites to celebrate the birth of his first son in the middle of the 16th century. The matsuri's main attraction is the kite-flying competition in the daytime and the parade of floats in the evening. Eighty-three floats cruise around the town, carrying musical bands playing hayashi music. The distinctive music called the kabuki hayashi also characterizes this festival.

【浜松まつり公式ウェブサイト】
Hamamatsu Matsuri official website
- http://hamamatsu-daisuki.net/matsuri/

巨大な凧も揚がる「凧揚げ合戦」。

A host of kites, including some that are quite enormous, adorn the sky in the competition.

京都祇園祭
きょうと ぎ おん まつり

Kyoto Gion Matsuri

開催時期・期間：毎年7月1〜31日　規模：およそ40万人　開催場所：京都府京都市

Dates: July 1 - 31, held annually　**Estimated number of spectators:** 400,000
Place: Kyoto City, Kyoto Prefecture

日本三大祭の一つとして有名なこの祭りの起源は869年にさかのぼる。見どころの「山鉾巡行」では32基の大きな山鉾が独特の「祇園囃子」の演奏に乗って順次市中を進む。曲がり角では、青竹を敷いて水をまき、音方向転換の技が披露される。もう一つの見どころ「神幸祭」では勇壮な神輿が市中を渡御する。

The Kyoto Gion Matsuri, one of Japan's three most prominent festivals, dates back to 869. In the Yamahoko Junkou (grand procession), thirty-two floats churn their ways through the town, accompanied by the distinctive tunes of the Gion Bayashi. When a yamahoko, which is not designed to turn, needs to turn a corner, thin bamboo strips are laid on the street and ample water is sprayed, then the people can demonstrate their skill in turning the lofty float. Another attraction is the Shinkosai, in which gorgeous mikoshi are carried throughout the town.

【祇園祭 "有料観覧席"】
Kyoto City Tourism Association
(for seat reservation)

- https://www.kyokanko.or.jp/gion/kanran.html

山鉾巡行をゆっくりと見ることができるのが有料観覧席。

■月日：7月17日［山鉾巡行］■観覧席設置場所：御池通　■料金：3180円（全席指定・パンフレット付）■お問い合せ：京都市観光協会 ☎075-752-0227

Seat reservations are available for those who want to thoroughly enjoy the Yamahoko Junko．
■Date: July 17th　■Place: Oike Street
■Charge: 3,180 yen, including a pamphlet, all seats are for reservation　■Contact: Kyoto City Tourism Association ☎075-752-0227

先頭と最後で巡行に約90分の差が出る山鉾巡行。
It takes 90 minutes to see the whole grand procession.

天神祭
てんじんまつり
Tenjin Matsuri

開催時期・期間：毎年7月24〜25日　規模：およそ130万人　開催場所：大阪府大阪市
Dates: July 24 - 25, held annually　**Estimated number of spectators:** 1,300,000
Place: Osaka City, Osaka Prefecture

祭りの始まりは大阪天満宮（おおさかてんまんぐう）が最初に祀（まつ）られた翌々年951年といわれる。見どころは「陸渡御（りくとぎょ）」と「船渡御（ふなとぎょ）」。陸渡御は、神事にしたがって御鳳輦（ごほうれん）に神霊を移し、御鳳輦と神輿や山車、3000人もの人々が一緒に大川まで渡御する。船渡御は、御鳳輦を載せた船をはじめとして100隻の船が大川へ漕ぎ出す。また、現代ではこの時にたくさんの花火が打ち上げられる。天神祭の神輿は鳳神輿と玉神輿の2基でどちらも古い歴史を持つ。

The history of the Tenjin Matsuri is said to date back to 951, two years after the foundation of the Osaka Tenmangu Shrine. The festival's main events are the Rikutogyo (land procession) and the Funatogyo (boat procession). The Rikutogyo starts with the kami moved onto the gohouren palanquin, which is carried down to the Okawa River accompanied by mikoshi, dashi and as many as 3,000 people. The gohouren is then moved onto a boat and descends the river along with 100 other boats. In recent years fireworks add to the festivity during the Funatogyo. During the matsuri two mikoshi also make their appearance. The Ohtori Mikoshi, with a phoenix on its rooftop, and the Tama Mikoshi, with a sacred gem (houju), both enjoy historical value.

【天神祭総合情報サイト】
Tenjin Matsuri information
- http://www.tenjinmatsuri.com/

天神祭の鳳神輿と玉神輿。

The Ohtori Mikoshi and Tama Mikoshi.

西条まつり
Saijo Matsuri

開催時期・期間：毎年10月14日〜16日　規模：およそ19万人　開催場所：愛媛県西条市

Dates: October 14 - 16, held annually　**Estimated number of spectators:** 190,000
Place: Saijo City, Ehime Prefecture

嘉母神社、石岡神社、伊曽乃神社、飯積神社が執り行なう秋の大祭が西条まつりで、それぞれの神社が次々と祭礼を行う。この中でも特に賑やかなのは伊曽乃神社の例大祭で、14日の前夜祭から山車の一種である「だんじり」が市内で巡行を始める。15日・16日は早朝の宮出しから夕方の宮入りまで見どころが多い。80基のだんじりが一斉に加茂川に入り、神輿が川を渡る。大きな太鼓台も登場し、これらが伊勢音頭の演奏で巡行する。

【西条まつり】
Saijo Matsuri website
- http://www.saijomatsuri.jp/

The Saijo Matsuri is a series of autumnal festivals presided by the Kamo Shrine, the Ishioka Shrine, the Isono Shrine, and the Izumi Shrine. Particularly exuberant is the festival of the Isono Shrine. The floats called danjiri appear on the street from the evening of October 14th. The following two days see a number of events, starting with each mikoshi's departure from the shrine early in the morning until their return in the evening. The matsuri culminates when all eighty danjiri go into the Kamo River to watch over each mikoshi's crossing of the stream. Large taikodai floats also move around the city, boosting the mood by playing the folk ballad, Ise Ondo.

加茂川にだんじりが入って行く。
A load of danjiri go into the river all at once.

日田祇園祭
(ひたぎおんまつり)

Hita Gion Matsuri

開催時期・期間：7月下旬頃の土・日　規模：およそ6万人　開催場所：大分県日田市(おおいたけんひたし)

Dates: Saturday and Sunday in late July, held annually
Estimated number of spectators: 60,000
Place: Hita City, Oita Prefecture

日田ではおよそ500年前から祇園が祀られていたと伝えられ、1665年には山鉾の記録がある。18世紀の初めには現在のような豪華な山鉾が巡行していた。現在は国指定重要無形民俗文化財となっている。見どころは「曳山行事(ひきやま)」と呼ばれる8基の山鉾の曳き回し。この山鉾は4つの車輪の上に台車が組まれ、そこに4本の柱を立て、人形や館の模型を飾りつけてあり「岩組山(いわくみやま)」と呼ばれる。上にいくほど大きくなる山鉾が、町の中を巡行する。

【日田祇園について】
Hita Gion information
- https://www.hita.ne.jp/~city/west/gio/gion.htm

The kami of Gion is said to have been enshrined in Hita 500 years ago. There is a record of yamahoko in a document dated back to 1665, and the opulent yamahoko procession was already taking place in the beginning of the 18th century. Today, the Hita Gion is designated as a significant intangible folk cultural asset of Japan. The festival's main event is the Hikiyama Gyoji, in which eight yamahoko floats are pulled around the town. On the four-wheeled foundation are standing four pillars, which are decorated with human figures and castle-like objects. The towering yamahoko with decorations protruding near the top, are admired by local people and visitors alike.

人形や館の模型を飾りつけた山鉾が巡行する。

The yamahoko with human figures and miniature structures go around the town.

伊万里トンテントン祭り
Imari Tontenton Matsuri

開催時期・期間：毎年10月22〜24日　　規模：およそ3万人　　開催場所：佐賀県伊万里市
Dates: October 22 - 24, held annually　　**Estimated number of spectators:** 30,000
Place: Imari City, Saga Prefecturere

　この祭りは、伊万里川河畔にある伊萬里神社の祭りで「伊万里供日」とも呼ばれる。神輿が巡行途中でぶつかり合う「合戦」が見どころで、日本三大けんか祭りの一つと数えられる。巡行では荒神輿が先に立ち団車が続き、打ち鳴らされる太鼓の音とともに「チョウサンヤ」「アラヨーイトナ」という掛け声を掛ける。合戦では神輿が取っ組み合い、そのまま川に落ち、先に川から上がった方が勝ちとなる。現在は安全に考慮し「合戦」を見合わせている。

【伊万里トンテントン】
[Imari Tontenton]
- http://ww7.tiki.ne.jp/~syowfuw/tontenton1.html

The Imari Tontenton Matsuri of the Imari Shrine situated by the Imari River is also known as the Imari Kunchi and is one of the three major fighting festivals in Japan. The matsuri features rough skirmishes between the mikoshi and floats during the procession. The so-called ara-mikoshi (rough mikoshi) is chased by the floats, dansha, and go around the town with energetic shouts and drum beats. The matsuri's climax is marked by the kawaotoshi, or the river fight, in which the mikoshi and the dansha engage in head-on grappling until both fall into the river. The one that is pulled ashore first is considered the winner. The fighting part, however, has been suspended recently in consideration of safety.

「キーワエンカ」の掛け声とともに神輿がぶつかる。

A wild clash of the mikoshi with the shout of provocation, "Kee wa enka!".

那覇大綱挽まつり
Naha Otsunahiki Matsuri

開催時期・期間：毎年体育の日の前日日曜日　　規模：およそ70万人　　開催場所：沖縄県那覇市

Dates: the Sunday before Sports Day, held annually　　**Estimated number of spectators:** 700,000
Place: Naha City, Okinawa Prefecture

琉球王国時代の伝統を引き継ぐ祭りで、現在は「大綱挽」前日に「市民演芸・民俗伝統芸能パレード」が行なわれる。「大綱挽」は、それぞれ長さ100m、直径1m56cmの女綱と男綱が、西と東から旗頭に導かれて「大綱挽行列」を行ない、次に2本の綱がつながれて、綱に取りつけられた7mの手綱が256本を持って壮大な綱引きが行なわれる。大綱はギネスブックで世界一のわら綱にも認められている。

【那覇大綱挽保存会】
Naha Otsunahiki Preservation Association

- http://www.naha-otsunahiki.org/

The Naha Otsunahiki, or the Giant Tug-of-War, finds its origin in the Ryukyu Kingdom. The tug-of-war is preceded by the citizens' parade, demonstrating local performing arts on the day before. The tug-of-war involves two enormous ropes of 100 meters in length and 156 centimeters in diameter. The two ropes, one representing men, and the other, women, are brought in from the east and west led by flag-bearers and tied together. People hold onto 256 thinner ropes that are tied to the giant ropes and start the massive tug-of-war. The giant ropes have been certified by the Guinness Book of World Records as the world's largest straw ropes.

つながれた女綱と男綱を西と東で引き合う。

The male and female ropes are tied together and pulled to the east and west.

❖ 参考文献

『江戸神輿』小澤宏之 著／講談社

『王妃マリー・アントワネット「美の肖像」』
家庭画報 編／世界文化社

『技術シリーズ 金工』金丸峯雄 編／朝倉書店

『最後の職人神輿師
　──六代目伊豆守則直の技と道具──』
吉羽和夫 著／河出書房新社

『彫金 手づくりのアクセサリー』
望月正子 著／主婦と生活社

『東京の宮神輿 春夏編』
戎光祥出版編集部 編／戎光祥出版

『日本の漆器』荒川浩和 他著／読売新聞社

『復活日本──黄金大神輿──
東京深川・富岡八幡宮御本社神輿──』
本田嘉郎 著／ぎょうせい

『ほんものの漆器 買い方と使い方』
荒川浩和 他著／新潮社

『神輿（NHK美の壺）』
NHK「美の壺」制作班 編／日本放送出版協会

『神輿（1）』監修恒夫 著／刊々堂出版社

『木工──指物技法』
秋岡芳夫 著／美術出版社

『木工具・使用法』秋岡芳夫 監修／創元社

『木彫入門』渡辺一生 著／文研出版

❖ 監修者紹介

宮本卯之助商店七代目
宮本卯之助

1941年東京浅草生まれ。明治大学商学部卒業。1975年神輿・太鼓の製造販売業を継ぎ、宮本卯之助商店第七代目店主となる。

株式会社 宮本卯之助商店

文久元年（1861年）創業。神輿・御宮・神社仏閣太鼓・祭礼山車太鼓・民俗芸能太鼓・能楽、長唄、雅楽器・祭礼具の製造販売、神輿・太鼓の修理、復元およびレンタルを業務とする。

本社：〒111-0032 東京都台東区浅草6-1-15
Tel：03-3873-4155　Fax：03-3875-6602
http://www.miyamoto-unosuke.co.jp/

❖ About the editorial supervisor

Miyamoto Unosuke

The seventh owner of the Miyamoto Unosuke Shoten. Born in 1941 in the Asakusa district in Tokyo. Graduated from Meiji University School of Commerce. Took over the family business in 1975 to become the seventh proprietor of the Miyamoto Unosuke Shoten, which sells mikoshi and taiko (Japanese drums).

Miyamoto Unosuke Shoten Co., Ltd.

Founded in 1861. Main lines of business include the production and sale of the mikoshi, household Shinto altars, taiko for shrines and temples, taiko for festival floats and for folk performing arts, musical instruments for the gagaku (ancient Japanese court music), and ritual articles. Also provides repair, reproduction and rental services of mikoshi and taiko.

Address: 6-1-15 Asakusa, Taito Ward,
Address: Tokyo, 111-0032
Tel: 03-3873-4155　Fax: 03-3875-6602
http://www.miyamoto-unosuke.co.jp/

●STAFF

編集	岩間靖典
執筆協力	岩間靖典／横須賀美也子／辻 慶太郎
写真協力	池田麻理／株式会社宮本卯之助商店
本文イラスト	ファクトリー・ウォーター
英文翻訳	岡本直子／Richard Hubbard
英文校正	福田篤人
装丁・本文デザイン	谷元将泰

Japanese-English Bilingual Books

神輿の歴史・鑑賞知識から、各地のお祭り情報まで
英語訳付き 日本の神輿と祭りハンドブック
The Japanese Portable Shrine and Festival Handbook

2015年7月13日　発　行　　　　　　　　　　　　NDC 386

監　修	宮本卯之助
発行者	小川雄一
発行所	株式会社 誠文堂新光社
	〒113-0033　東京都文京区本郷3-3-11
	（編集）電話03-5805-7285
	（販売）電話03-5800-5780
	http://www.seibundo-shinkosha.net/
印　刷	株式会社 大熊整美堂
製　本	和光堂 株式会社

©2015, Seibundo Shinkosha Publishing Co.,Ltd.　　　　　　　Printed in Japan

検印省略／禁・無断転載
落丁・乱丁本はお取り替え致します。

本書のコピー、スキャン、デジタル化等の無断複製は、著作権法上での例外を除き、禁じられています。本書を代行業者等の第三者に依頼してスキャンやデジタル化することは、たとえ個人や家庭内での利用であっても著作権法上認められません。

R〈日本複製権センター委託出版物〉本書を無断で複写複製（コピー）することは、著作権法上での例外を除き、禁じられています。本書をコピーされる場合は、事前に日本複製権センター（JRRC）の許諾を受けてください。
JRRC〈http://www.jrrc.or.jp／　E-mail：jrrc_info@jrrc.or.jp　電話03-3401-2382〉

ISBN978-4-416-71548-2